Cover art by JANE EVANS

Initiation into Yoga

An Introduction to the Spiritual Life

by Sri Krishna Prem

with a foreword by Sri Madhava Ashish

A QUEST BOOK

published by

The Theosophical Publishing House
Wheaton, Ill., U.S.A.
Madras, India / London, England

First Quest edition, 1976

Published by the Theosophical Publishing House, Wheaton, Illinois, a depart-
ment of the Theosophical Society in
America.

Library of Congress Cataloging in Publication Data

Sri Krishna Prem, 1898-1965.
    Initiation into yoga.

    (Quest book)
    1. Yoga. I. Title.
B132.Y6S7 1976   181'.45
ISBN 0-8356-0484-5 pbk.   76-10790

Printed in the United States of America

Contents

Foreword: Sri Krishna Prem through the eyes of a disciple

In the present day extraordinary dress is no longer the sign of an extraordinary man: it is the fashion to wear weird clothes. India is flooded with foreign freaks in various stages of dress and undress, hairy and shorn, many, with greater or less sincerity, adopting the role of the wandering mendicant monk, the *sannyāsi* or *sādhū*. In the 1920s, however, when Ronald Nixon (later to become Sri Krishna Prem) came to India to teach at Lucknow University, the number of Europeans who broke through the restraints of the Sahib's social solidarity could be counted on the fingers of one hand. A white skin in Indian dress was more often a grotesque parody, the unhappy victim of leucoderma, a disease that destroys the pigment in the skin.

By 1942, when I reached India, the system of social restraints was beginning to crack. The Old Guard could no longer control the behaviour of the thousands of young Englishmen who swarmed over the sub-continent on wartime tasks. Through the cracks some of us found our way into the strange world of Indian saints, semi-saints, and downright frauds. We found ourselves afloat without a compass on an ocean to which we had no charts, where the winds of the spirit blew the fortunate to port and the unfortunate sank. But though I met Europeans who had taken to the Indian manner of living, and though I had myself at times worn Indian dress, in four years I never set eyes on any non-Indian who had taken the plunge into orthodox Indian *sannyās*.

When Sri Krishna Prem strode barefoot on to the verandah of Almora's one Western-style hotel where I was having a very English tea with a very English old lady, the apparition fitted none of my categories, so I retired to watch from behind a self-protective grin. Six foot, big-boned but soft-fibred, blue-eyed, a high-domed shaven head with a stubble of white hair, and a lot of that pinko-white Anglo-Saxon skin that goes red in the sun showing in the

gaps of his ochre garments: it was a remarkable if not startling
appearance. A man in his late forties, he seemed to be entirely at
ease in himself and to assume that others would be similarly so, in
spite of the discrepancy between his dress and the setting he had
entered.

He talked: brilliantly, learnedly, wittily. It was an impressive
show, and I recognized the professionalism of the man who has
trained himself to hold the attention of a class of students or a group
of questioners. Two of us was too small an audience, and the eerie
blue eyes turned from one to the other, looking through, not at one.
Later I grew fearful of those eyes, having learned that they really did
look through one. For the moment, I was on guard with bared
teeth, and, though I admired his evident learning, I felt his intellect
rise up between us like polished armour. I had not met the man.

I had first heard of him some three years earlier while on vacation
in Ranikhet, a military cantonment in the Himalayan foothills
thirty miles from Almora. The British still referred to him by his
English name, Nixon, and coupled it with that of Alexander, his
friend and disciple. My host described them as 'two Cambridge
intellectuals living in the interior. And they dislike visitors.' Then,
in Calcutta, I ran across a few people who had visited the ashram,
and I heard somewhat derogatory comments: they were 'intellectuals', 'ritualists', 'orthodox Hindus', 'devotees'. Yet it seemed that
all had been impressed and were trying to depotentialize the chal-
lenge of what they had seen by taking a deprecatory attitude. I was
left with the impression that Krishna Prem was something to be
reckoned with.

As I have said, however, we were afloat without a compass. We
followed our noses, and some noses were put out of joint by Krishna
Prem's flagrant violation of the then accepted code of British supe-
riority. He had 'gone native', but done it in such a superior way that
no British mud flung at him would stick. He had done his share of
fighting in the First World War. He was a successful professor of
English literature, much loved and admired by his Indian students.
His disciple and companion, Major Alexander, was a highly quali-
fied physician in the Indian Medical Service whose premature
retirement as Principal of the Lucknow Medical College had upset

the Lucknow public. Krishna Prem's guru, Sri Yashoda Mai, was Mrs Chakravarti, wife of the ex-Vice-Chancellor of Lucknow University.

With the end of the war in the Far East, my job as a civilian aircraft technician crawled to a finish. Roads led in many directions. I was twenty-six and had four months' leave to my credit. To give myself time to decide whether life might offer more than just another job, I set out for Almora. There, cheap, quiet accommodation in scattered bungalows facing the Himalayan peaks, far from military cantonments, had attracted a number of Western people whose eccentricities had earned for the area the name 'Cranks' Ridge'.

They were elderly people who shared a wide range of interests: art, literature, religion; and they wished to live quietly. Their intelligence was of a high order and their experience of life full and varied. In their youth they might have passed through periods of starry-eyed enthusiasm and blind devotion, but now each in his own way was solidly devoted to a somewhat amorphous 'path' which was distilled from all the public religious teachings. All encouraged me in my groping enquiries but none attempted to enlist me in his particular 'thing'. And I found, whenever I pressed a question beyond the limits of their experience, that each would quietly and benignly reply, 'When Sri Krishna Prem returns, ask him.'

Sri Krishna Prem was away in the plains and would soon return to the ashram. Since his guru's death two years earlier he was the head of it. The ashram was not on Cranks' Ridge but twenty miles away by bridle path on the other side of a deep valley, a white spot high up on a wooded hill. A few of the community of cranks knew Krishna Prem well but the others had only a slight acquaintance with him, and this made their separately repeated advice all the more impressive. By the time he arrived I was ready to look on him as a demi-god, but by the end of that first meeting on the hotel verandah I was not at all sure that my friends were right.

Another afternoon tea in Almora marked my first meeting with Moti Rani, Krishna Prem's first disciple and the youngest daughter of his guru. She was short and fat, with a typically round Bengali head, dark-skinned, poor features by the canons of Indian beauty, but magnificent eyes, fine skin, and hands that artists wanted to borrow. Her feet, deformed at birth, had been straightened out by treatment and looked normal enough, but she walked with a waddle and might fall over like a tin soldier at the slightest provocation. Her brief marriage had ended with her finding her husband another wife, and then, after her father's death, she had made her home at her mother's ashram. Krishna Prem, who had known her since she was 'a little girl in a pink frock', was her 'little father' and she treated him with an affectionate familiarity which made it plain that his glittering intellectual armour was not invulnerable.

They seemed an oddly assorted pair to be travelling together: Krishna Prem in his rough and ill-washed homespun cotton, shaving only on Mondays and Fridays, feet calloused and cracked, imperturbably sitting like a sacred bull on a city pavement and puffing at a pipe, his one un-*sādhū*-like luxury in which, as he said, he smoked not tobacco but matches; and Moti in Benares-embroidered silk saree, with bobbed hair and jewellery, delicate, dynamic, vivacious, and the centre of attention as by right.

Within ten minutes of our meeting, Moti was teasing me about a recalcitrant forelock which the dry hill air had made unmanageable. I made a shamefaced excuse and tried to sink out of sight behind a row of brightly coloured cushions, only to find them stuffed with pine needles. Esther Merston, an elderly English lady who was my hostess on the ridge, kept up a running chatter of rarefied intellection in her precise, opiniated way. In the pauses Moti would return to that damned forelock with a giggling 'But tell me why you don't cut it off'. When my tormentor desisted, I heard Esther inviting herself along with me to a week's stay at the ashram.

During the week we waited before making our trip, Krishna Prem's friend, variously known as Major Robert Dudley Alexander, I.M.S., Doctor Sahib, or, more familiarly, Bob, passed by on pilgrimage to Badrinath, an ancient temple in the high Himalayas. Almost as tall as Krishna Prem, with blue eyes deep-set behind shaggy eyebrows, lean and bony, he was bounding along on the balls of his bare feet to cover a hundred and twenty miles each way in the next fortnight. Just after the First World War he and Ronald Nixon had met in a Cambridge bookshop, both hunting for one of

H. P. Blavatsky's theosophical works. 'At that instant,' Bob said, 'I felt I had met a man I could follow for the rest of my life.' Follow him he did, though his long medical course delayed his coming to India till the year Nixon took *sannyas* and became Sri Krishna Prem. And, as Yashoda Mai foretold at their first meeting, it was another ten years before Bob was ready to join the ashram.

Bob had covered the distance from the ashram to Almora in five hours. It took my hostess and me the best part of nine; elderly Esther on Almora's one, elderly horse, and me trying to emulate the odd Englishmen of the ashram by going barefoot. It was a tiring journey, nine miles down one side of the valley and nine miles of unremitting climb up the other, a hot, dusty bridle path, winding past terraces of rubble soil where women were harvesting yellow millet and scarlet cockscomb. Then the road led up into pine forest which changed to oak where the air grew cold and thin.

Krishna Prem had laughingly directed us to take the 'Middle Path' which avoided the steepest part of the climb, but we missed it in a maze of cow tracks and eventually arrived at a lonely, crumbling building high on the hill, where two well-kept dogs barked furiously at our intrusion. A man who emerged from the building grudgingly admitted that they belonged to the ashram and led us down past dilapidated terraces towards a temple dome that was now showing through the trees.

In general I am sympathetic to the idea that first impressions are significant. During this period, however, either my small intuitive faculty was dormant or the new impressions were too strange and numerous for me to handle. I was suspicious of Krishna Prem, abashed by Moti, and now I was repelled by the dead grey cement of the temple dome, the rusted iron roofing of an upper storey that leaned against it, and the brown-painted verandahs clad with iron sheet weather-proofing. It was drab. But the drab temple rose from an eight-feet-high sea of flowering cosmos and marigolds, a garden that had run wild.

We were put up in a stone-roofed bungalow, called the 'School' from the time when Krishna Prem's guru taught village children reading, writing, and the elements of English, which were then the keys to employment. Now it was used as a guest house, but guests were few. The place smelled of damp cedar-wood and was crowded with bits of furniture not wanted elsewhere, pictures no one wanted to look at, and old magazines no one wanted to read.

I had heard so much about their rigid orthodoxy at the ashram that I hesitated to approach the temple proper lest I be chased away as an untouchable, so my first view of the evening service was from a distance. The din of gongs, bells and a kettle-drum was strangely stirring, as was the half-glimpsed form of Krishna Prem offering the symbols of the elements amidst clouds of incense. The inner shrine was lit up like a glowing cave in the October night. And then the lights and incense were carried out to be offered at the newly constructed *samādhi* which housed the ashes of the guru and founder of the ashram.

After the evening service they sang in the temple ante-room, Krishna Prem leading and accompanying himself on a small harmonium, and Moti repeating each line of the song as is the custom in such communal singing. This was a different man; the intellectual barriers were down and emotion flooded him and throbbed through the temple. It was not the cheap, hysterical, auto-excitation one finds in many hymn-singing communities. It was the outpouring of an individual soul in longing for union with the divine beloved. There were times when he would lose himself in song and then sit in the numinous silence until normal consciousness returned. Later I heard from Moti how he had been known to leap up and dance till he fell senseless. My reaction on these early occasions was to curl up inside myself lest my own inhibited feelings dare show themselves.

There followed a long wait on a draughty upper verandah while Krishna Prem first performed his *sandhya*, the major daily Hindu practice, and then prepared the evening meal. We had to retire from the verandah while the food was carried past to the temple, lest we defile it with hungry looks. After another long wait, while the ritual offerings were performed, we were at last invited to eat – a simple meal of chapattis made from local flour, a dish of potatoes and a little milk.

There are few things that upset the whole being of a man so much as deprivation of food or irregular and unaccustomed mealtimes. The old world, and India is still part of it, with its religious fasts and only the sun for a clock, kept the digestive system flexible. I had been one of those unfortunate brats who collapse from hunger at early-morning chapel at school. Now I was given ample opportunity for resentment against this calm man, Krishna Prem, who seemed indifferent to what he ate or even whether he ate at all. After rising at five so as to bathe before the morning service, one was kept waiting for tea until Krishna Prem finished his morning meditation, which might last until ten. Supper came after his evening meditation and the temple offerings. Only the main midday meal was reasonably on time. Moti, who liked to treat even the making of a cup of tea as an adventure, found my irritability over delayed meals intolerable. Until food had been offered to Sri Krishna in the temple, and until the guru was ready, no member of the ashram was supposed to take so much as a sip of water. With swimming head and grumbling stomach I sullenly obeyed, because there was no alternative except to leave.

During this first visit there was a lot of talk about the temple, which Krishna Prem represented as a magical point of interaction between this world and the powers of divinity, inspiring harmony and fanning the flame of the spirit in men's hearts. The symbols and rituals of worship magically invoked the presence of divinity and stirred resonances within their human witnesses. He said the circular, integrating motion of the offerings around the images on the altar corresponded to the integrating movement of thought around the divinity within the human heart; and he spoke of the integrating effects of actions dedicated to the divine and centred on the temple images.

I had met people who fervently assured me that all things could be controlled by words of power, if only they knew them; that misfortunes could be averted by the wearing of certain jewels, though they suffered misfortune; and, while their eyes bulged, that bowel washes were the cure for all bodily and spiritual ills; and they all seemed just a little bit off it. They were fanatics, persuading others of what they themselves secretly doubted or substituting physical correlates for their psychic antecedents. But Krishna Prem was not a missionary. He did not attempt to persuade me or anyone else that he held the keys to these or any other mysteries. He did not try to hold me with a glittering eye, nor did his eyes bulge, nor did he grow fervent and inarticulate. If one challenged a statement that seemed extravagant, he supported it with examples taken from experience, without mystery-mongering or laying claim to superior knowledge. Unlike most religious instructors, when he did not know the answer to a question, he simply said, 'I don't know.' Wherever one touched the man he rang true.

At this distance in time, over twenty-five years, I cannot exactly reproduce either his words or even the ideas he expressed. As the years progressed, his ideas changed and matured. But at that time I was not looking for perfection. Two years earlier I had seen the South Indian saint Ramana Maharshi, the radiance of whose attainment was almost visible, but he was too far removed from my muddled state for me to relate his teaching to the practical necessities of living. At that time I did not see in Krishna Prem what I had seen in Ramana, but perhaps it was just because of this that I felt close enough to him for his words to have practical application. For me, tired of the clamour of military aircraft engines and the petty intrigues of my colleagues, tired of war and disillusioned of my British heritage, Krishna Prem's portrayal of an ultimately meaningful life was uplifting. He was conjuring up glowing images, opening new worlds to my view. But was it true? Was he articulating his experience, or was he just playing with glittering words?

Sitting on an outcrop of rock beside the temple one morning, he was answering some of the questions I had saved up to ask him. Then I challenged him. 'What,' I asked, 'does all this mean to you, to you yourself?' He was silent for a moment, and the flush that came to his face made his eyes seem even more blue. He gave me a very simple, straight answer. I have never remembered what he said on that occasion. Perhaps I hardly heard the words, because it came to me with a shock that I had got through his outer armour and, for a moment, seen the man behind. It was the sort of man I had never seen before: simple, in the sense of uncomplicated, clean, soft and sunlike. I was torn between embarrassment at my intrusion, and desire to feast my soul on such rare beauty. For the next few days I felt like the country bumpkin of legend who stumbled into fairyland.

Moti did one of her tin soldier acts, spraining her knee, and I was appointed her mobile walking stick. At thirty she was already a sick woman, destined to die from kidney disease within five years. But despite this and a host of minor ailments she was vibrantly alive. At first one saw her as a laughing, teasing, vivacious girl and wondered what this colourful person was doing in the remote Himalayas. Her spirit was mercurial, leaping from laughter to anger, from gentle wheedling to imperious command. She would read Plato with as much zest as she read *Winnie-the-Pooh*, and I have seen her rout Krishna Prem and a professor of philosophy in philosophical argument, primarily capping her victory with 'I got a gold medal for logic at school'. Just as Krishna Prem hid behind intellectual armour, Moti hid the beauty of her nature behind a screen of laughter. Like Jalal-ud-din Rumi's, her jokes were not jokes, they were teachings.

It took me a long time to come to terms with this side of Moti and to understand why Krishna Prem was as devoted to his guru's daughter as he had been to his guru. Though Krishna Prem was head of the ashram, expounded the teaching, and had won public acclaim as author, devotee, and man of considerable attainment, Moti, with her Hindu birthright, managed the day-to-day affairs. This was acceptable: the great man needed someone to look after worldly details while his mind roamed free in the infinite. What was not so easily acceptable was that Moti produced emotionally charged situations which compelled one to practise the teachings which Krishna Prem had articulated in relative calm.

So great is the split between ideas and their implementation that few people understood what was happening. We all admired Krishna Prem and we all loved Moti. Yet we all found Moti a very difficult person to live with. In fact, I knew only one man who saw the point in her behaviour. That was Dr Boshi Sen, a famous Indian scientist living in Almora. Once when Moti was bludgeoning me with one of her tantrums in his presence he laughed delightedly at a sight that was enough to embarrass or even to frighten most men. His own guru had treated him in a similar way.

Moti had exceptional capacities in the realm of psychic phenomena, and I once spoke to her regretfully of my own lack in this field. 'What do you want with these things?' she replied. 'They are crooked, deceitful and womanly, like the moon. Try to become more like Krishna Prem. In him I see the straightness and trueness of the sun.' Yet there is no denying the beauty and fascination of the moon. Moti's inner beauty might at times have been shrouded by storm clouds, but the longer I knew her, the more I became aware that her passionate nature was utterly dedicated to the spirit, regardless of what it cost her. If she undertook to help someone on his path, she would spare neither herself nor him in the effort to change his nature, 'shatter it to bits and then remould it nearer to the heart's desire'. Though the modes were different, it was the same aspiration that flamed in both Krishna Prem and Moti: a rapier in the hands of Krishna Prem, a scimitar in Moti's. And in both of them laughter bubbled like a spring of clear, refreshing water.

However, none of this was shown to me until I was well and truly hooked. For the moment I was dazed and disoriented. The winds had blown the castaway to shore on the islands of the blessed. It was a magic island above the clouds, a dream, and the dream might end: Moti started to knit me a pullover.

Esther and I visited more friends in the neighbourhood and we then planned to travel south, ending our journey at Ramana Maharshi's ashram in South India where I would decide the future course of my life – or so I thought. But Esther needed a fortnight to settle her affairs, so she suggested that I return to Krishna Prem's ashram for that period. Krishna Prem, the reputed hater of visitors, agreed.

After a fifty-mile trek through the crystal-clear air of the October hills I reached the ashram to be scolded by Moti for not sending her a telepathic message. The pullover was ready. I think she had knitted me into it. At the end of the fortnight I was given permission to stay on indefinitely.

The little ashram was filling up with the four or five visitors it took to fill it, and Bob was back from Badrinath. I now occupied a six-foot by eight-foot cell on the ground floor of the temple, but though closer to the life of the ashram I was also more excluded because most of the talk was in Bengali which Krishna Prem talked fluently, to the delight of his Bengali friends. I noticed that he slipped into a more feeling mode of expression when talking Bengali than when conversing in English. And he seemed able to adapt himself to the needs of people, communicating with a simple old peasant woman as easily as he did with a sophisticated intellectual. He had gained a reputation for his knowledge of Sanskrit, which he said he did not deserve because he did not know the language well but simply made good use of the little he did know. He had studied Pali at Cambridge where he first became interested in Buddhism as a branch of Theosophy and had taken a Buddhist initiation. There he had filled his rooms with Buddhist paraphernalia, including a Chinese Buddha image and Tibetan T'ankas given him by his father who mildly encouraged his eldest son's exotic tastes. His Christian Scientist mother found his rooms too full of 'confusion' to suit her.

One heard much about Cambridge. The post-war years at King's College gave him and his friends occasion for a rich expansion of interests. They were not immature youths straight from school, but men whose manhood had been thrust early upon them by the hardships and stresses of war. Perhaps it is natural for intelligent men to turn from enforced contemplation of death to a search for the meaning of life. Whatever the reason might be, there was a group of friends linked by a community of interests which showed itself in their joining various branches of the Theosophical Society and, allied movements, Buddhist, Masonic, the Liberal Catholic Church and a healing group that broke up abruptly when a number of their 'patients' died. And then there was the 'Airy Fairy Lilian' who ran an occult meditation group, building thought forms and sending members on astral journeys. Whichever movement they joined, they lit their lamps at its flame and then carried them through life, some brightly, some dimly, but they all seem to have stayed alight.

These men were in some sense pioneers of the present world-wide movement that sends thousands of people searching in exotic faiths for a spiritually meaningful interpretation of existence. Like them, Ronald Nixon was in revolt against regimentation, against the senselessness of war, and against material values. Like them, he rejected the hollow promises of social reform and sought instead a personal solution to the problems of life. And, like many of them, he turned towards India, the land of the Buddha, of Apollonius of Tyana's mysterious Brahmans, of Alexander's Gymnosophists, of

the Masters of Blavatsky's Theosophical Society, of the Upanishads, and of Yoga.

From a non-conformist school at Taunton Ronald won an
Exhibition in science at King's College. But the war intervened and
he went up to Cambridge after demobilization from the Royal
Flying Corps. With his Exhibition, a government grant for inter-
rupted studies, and generous help from the college, he got through
his course without financial help from his family. His tutor told him
that the least important part of his life at Cambridge was attending
lectures, and Ronald took the advice seriously. It was not that he
did no work, but he was blessed with a photographic memory and
had only to read a book once to be able to recall where any passage
appeared. The unpleasantness of war had sated his appetite for
applied science. The college allowed him to change his course to the
mental and moral science tripos, and he sailed off with enthusiasm
into the world of philosophy and literature.

The event that seems to have marked the beginning of his inner
life was a visit to the British Museum where he was confronted by
the Chinese Lohan Buddha, then impressively placed in the main
entrance hall. In the utterly calm poise of that severe image he
sensed the reality of an attainment to which he could dedicate his
life. There was then still doubt as to the Buddha's historic, as
opposed to mythic, status. Ronald argued that historicity had no
necessary bearing on what was depicted in an image made hundreds
of years after the Buddha's death. An artist can project into his
medium only what is, or potentially is, in the human heart. If a man
can portray in an image the calm poise of the indrawn spirit, then
such a state is attainable by man. What can be attained, he went on
to argue, in endless time must have been attained, whether by the
Buddha or by someone else. What one man can attain, another can
attain. And so he set foot on the journey of the soul.

At the end of his time at Cambridge he sought some means of
getting to India where, he felt, one might yet find men who taught
from experience the way to the Buddha's world-transcending poise.
Applications for a teaching job in India led to his being interviewed
in London. The interviewer approved, gave dangerous advice on
the necessity of taking purgatives daily in the tropics, and advanced

the now penniless Ronald money for his fare to Lucknow where he was to be Reader in English at the university. 'These foreign appointments are all very well for people who have no home ties,' complained his mother. 'And the strength of those ties,' thought Ronald, 'is just why I have to go.'

From the moment of his arrival in Lucknow, Ronald fell in love with India and her people. Younger than many of his students, he associated with them and with his Indian colleagues, and he ignored the British community. Seeing that this behaviour would lead to the brilliant, irrepressible young professor being ostracized by the British, Dr Chakravarti, the Bengali Vice-Chancellor, invited Ronald to stay permanently in his guest-house. Chakravarti was himself an ardent Theosophist and deeply sympathized with Ronald's spiritual search.

Ronald's affinity for Indians and their way of life put him in an unusual position. An unwritten code ruled British society in India: newcomers were expected to adhere to the Establishment, live British, eat British, join the British club, and pay duty calls on any senior man from the immediate boss up to the Governor of the Province. Relationships with Indians were defined, crudely or subtly according to the class levels on either side. Anyone who went too far was cold-shouldered, black-balled from the club, abandoned by his British clients, or sent home by the next boat, depending on the power the community could wield over the individual. The system generally ensured that newcomers either conformed or left. Ronald did neither. His survival in the face of British disapproval was partly due to the Vice-Chancellor's patronage, for Dr Chakravarti was a friend of the State Governor, Sir Harcourt Butler, who was himself a highly unorthodox official. The British could not effectively complain at young Professor Nixon flouting their conventions. Yet anyone who has not seen India under the British Raj will have difficulty in appreciating the degree of independence and moral courage needed to withstand the coercive pressures of the system.

Ronald made many Indian friends. His shining countenance caught their imagination, and I still meet grey-haired old men whose faces light up when they talk of their Professor Nixon, even though they were members of a class of three hundred science students who attended Ronald's lectures only once a week. Their outstanding memory is of Ronald racing past at excessive speed on his motor-cycle. But so inexact is their memory of a mythologized Ronald that men who were his students when I was in the cradle have joyfully claimed me as their hero.

Ronald's strong individualism protected him from the influences which usually moulded young Englishmen into 'pukka Sahibs'. Sometimes, however, he ran foul of officialdom, once by cavalierly overtaking the Lucknow Superintendent of Police, also on a motor-cycle, an event that led to threats to have his passport cancelled. He was not aggressively rebellious, he simply went his own way. There was no venom in the man, so his British colleagues grew accustomed to his eccentricities. At Cambridge he had been a ready and ruthless debater; and since he never lost his temper, even under provocation, unfriendly taunts were apt to boomerang. Since he did not want to join the British club, the British could gain no satisfaction by black-balling him. Since he did not want their company, there was no point in ostracizing him. Since he was undeniably good at his job, they could not, with a Bengali as Vice-Chancellor, have him removed for failure to conform to British standards of racial discrimination. Since he treated them without rancour, they ended by being friendly enough.

Ronald spent his time studying Pali and Sanskrit, organizing student theatricals, and casting around in search of a spiritual teacher. His friendship with the Chakravarti family developed to the point where he was treated as an adopted son, and the longer he knew them, the more he came to appreciate the exceptional qualities of Dr Chakravarti and his wife. The tall, dignified Dr Chakravarti, whose blue eyes and fair skin made him look more like a Kashmiri than a Bengali, led a curiously double life. His personal quarters were furnished in Western style and his table was the same. He neither drank nor smoked. His inner life, which one might call Theosophicalized Hindu, was shared with only a small circle of friends. Throughout his life, wherever he might be staying, he rose at three and meditated until six in the morning. He had met Madame Blavatsky, joined the Theosophical Society, and became General Secretary of the Indian branch. Annie Besant was a close friend and was much influenced by him. His wife, Monica, had persuaded him to allow her to meet as many as possible of the spiritual figures of the day in pursuit of her own search, but had ended by asking initiation from him because, she said, she had found no one his equal.

Ronald once asked Chakravarti what sort of woman Blavatsky was. One would have had to know that fiery and tempestuous nature to appreciate his reply: 'I have known only one woman like her', and he nodded towards his wife who was sitting a few feet away. With one side of her nature Monica Chakravarti would mother anyone or anything that stirred her compassion, from men in trouble to an orphaned litter of puppies which she suckled. She played the social part of Mrs Vice-Chancellor with cultured refinement and entertained her husband's distinguished guests. On the other hand, she hob-nobbed with outlandish religious mendicants and had a fund of peasant woman's crude sayings that she could use to great effect. Unlike her husband, she held that if a man has anything of spiritual worth within him it will show on the outside. As a consequence, she neither hid her own lamp under a bushel of conventionalities, nor did she object to eccentricities of dress and behaviour in others seeking the same goal. Travelling in Europe with her husband and Annie Besant, she was mobbed by a crowd in St Peter's at Rome. Dark, big-eyed, beautiful, and wearing a blue saree embroidered with silver stars, she was taken for the Virgin Mary. The crowd tore pieces off her garment for sacred relics. Annie bustled her into a cab and admonished her never to wear that saree again. And, when dressed in all her finery at the Paris Exhibition of 1902, she was thought to be the Queen of Madagascar. Even Queen Victoria, seeing Monica from her coach at Windsor, sent her a summons to the Palace.

Ronald respected Dr Chakravarti highly, but he felt Mrs Chakravarti to be the greater of the two. The event which marked the beginning of his devotion to his guru occurred when he was spending a holiday with the Chakravarti family at Almora. Mrs Chakravarti agreed to teach him Hindi and made him read from a Hindi version of the life of Sri Krishna. As he read, she explained and commented. 'When she spoke of Sri Krishna,' he told me, 'it was as if Krishna was in the next room. One could not see him, but he was there.' A few months later Ronald asked her for initiation. Apart from insisting on vegetarianism, which is incumbent on members of the Krishna cult, she made only one condition: as she put it, he must 'stick'. The old Indian concept of self-dedication and obedience to the guru invested initiation with great seriousness. Under the influence of Theosophy, Europeans began seeking oriental initiations, but they did not appreciate the single-pointed loyalty expected of initiates. When the novelty of one initiation wore off, they would take another elsewhere. For this reason, Dr Chakravarti flatly refused initiation to several Europeans who applied to him. 'They don't stick,' he said, 'they expect to get something, put it in their pockets, and go back to Europe. This was the basis for his wife's stressing the point. Vegetarianism was no problem to Ronald who had been brought up that way by his mother.

About a year later Monica Chakravarti received an overwhelming vision of the unity of being which, to her, represented the culmination of her life's dedication to the spiritual path. The following day she sent a note to Ronald, written in Hindi: 'What you are seeking, that I have found.'

Dr Chakravarti's retirement in 1926 put Ronald in a position where he had to clarify his priorities. The Chakravartis were going to live in Benares. Ronald's Lucknow job was well paid and his now proven ability assured him a career, but if he stayed there he would seldom see his gurus. If he moved with his gurus, he would have to take a job at the Benares Hindu University at one-third his current salary. His colleagues advised him strongly against going. Dr and Mrs Chakravarti refused to influence his decision, but Chakravarti gave advice:'Whenever I have to make a major decision in my life,' he said, 'I try to follow what I feel to be highest in myself. I have not always succeeded. When I have, I have never had occasion to regret it. When I have not, I have always regretted it.' That was enough for Ronald and he went to Benares.

Eighteen months later doctors told Mrs Chakravarti that her lungs would not stand another hot season in the plains and she must go to the hills. To a motherly woman who had adopted forty children and had four of her own this was a severe blow. But it seems that the far-reaching effects of her vision were making it increasingly difficult to tolerate what, in contrast to her vision of Eternity, were the meaningless trivialities of family life. Because of high blood pressure her husband could not accompany her, and she therefore asked his permission to take monastic orders. If she had to leave home under such circumstances, she would leave it entirely and fulfil a lifelong ambition by building a temple to Sri Krishna and staying there in his service. Again faced with a decision between his career and his guru, this time Ronald did not hesitate but accompanied Mrs Chakravarti when she left. She chose to go to Almora where her husband had friends. As her guru, Dr Chakravarti invested her with the robes of the Vaishnava order of Vairagis, and she took the name Sri Yashoda Mai. Sri Yashoda Mai then inducted her disciple, Ronald Nixon, into the order and gave him the name Sri Krishna Prem. During the two years it took them to find and acquire a site for the temple Krishna Prem had to beg from door to door for food and to observe the strictest rules of Hindu orthodoxy. By 1930 they were settled in the ashram and within a year the temple was built and images of Sri Krishna and his consort, Radha, installed and consecrated. A handful of disciples collected, some of whom built cottages for themselves. Cultivated terraces provided most of their basic needs.

The discipline Yashoda Mai imposed on her followers was that of orthodox Hinduism, a system so complex and far-reaching that, if followed with sincerity, there is no single action, feeling, or thought that can be separated from the sacramental attitude towards living. Its practice can give rise to an acute sense of self-awareness, for one must be aware at all times of one's state of ritual purity. To be aware of it, one must be constantly watchful of even casual actions and contacts, and to maintain it one must be ready to take the appropriate purificatory measures. When the ashram was under several feet of snow, measures such as bathing were not the pleasurable relaxation that a ritual dip in a temple tank can be in the heat of the plains.

Yashoda Mai was not an easy taskmaster. She admitted to having had trouble with her temper when young, and even as a mature and elderly woman she could make a scene. Having seen the daughter blowing the roof off, I can imagine what the mother was like. However, she treated Krishna Prem with such consistent gentleness that he complained she was making things too easy for him. He had seen her treatment of others.

With warm-hearted motherliness Yashoda Mai would agree to some man settling at the ashram under her guidance and make all necessary arrangements for his well-being. But then she would, as Krishna Prem put it, turn the pressure on. Non-observance of the ashram rules, personal habits such as nose-picking, laziness, failure to show due respect to the guru, or even mistakes in ordinary speech, might call forth sharp criticism spiced with crude analogies. She hit below the belt, saying the things other people only think, as if the polite pretences of social custom did not exist. If anyone answered back, it was a signal for a detailed listing of his shortcomings which might culminate with his being told how distasteful it was for the deity to have such a loathsome creature about the place. Almost invariably the poor fellow would take his loathsomeness away. Krishna Prem never quite understood why she did it.

By ordinary standards Krishna Prem's life was not easy. The fact that he thought it was, when others thought it was not, may account for the reputation he gained for devotion to his guru. He was constantly at her side, nursing her in her increasingly frequent periods of illness, performing the temple rituals which included preparation of the ashram food, managing the ashram affairs, and expounding his guru's teaching to visitors. And in the long winter evenings he would read aloud while Yashoda Mai knitted, embroidered, or made carpets.

In 1930, when the temple was being built and Yashoda Mai was staying in a ramshackle cottage up the hill, Dr Alexander paid a visit. Yashoda Mai asked him to examine her and to give an estimate of her life expectancy. She was ill and wanted to know how much time she had to make something of her disciples. The doctor gave her two years at the outside, but she lived to have a chastened Alexander join the ashram eight years later and she died in 1944 after appointing Krishna Prem as her successor.

Krishna Prem accepted the responsibilities of both ashram and disciples, but he once told me he would have preferred the wandering life of the mendicant. I sometimes found him in a depressed mood, a fact that puzzled me until I noticed that these moods coincided with the approach of the holiday seasons when visitors and disciples were expected and he would have to submit to their demands for attention. There were few visitors in those days; the eighteen-mile walk deterred all but the most hardy.

I have indicated the complementary manner in which Krishna Prem and Moti Rani shared the responsibility for running the ashram, Krishna Prem teaching through speech and Moti through behaviour. I do not mean to suggest that Krishna Prem's teaching was theoretical. One of my earliest memories of the ashram is of sprawling in the afternoon sun on Moti's verandah. Krishna Prem had been sent a pamphlet of the sort scores of Indian *sādhūs* produce, expressing the writer's particular teaching or exhortation to society. He threw it across to me with a 'Take a look at that'.

When I had finished reading: 'Well,' he said, 'is it there?'

'Is what where?' I fumbled.

'The thing,' he said. 'Is the thing, the spirit, in that pamphlet?'

'How should I know?' I countered.

'But you *must* know. You must be able to recognize whether he is writing from experience or whether it is just words, hearsay.'

'Some of the things he says seem true,' I ventured.

The reply was devastating. 'One can't write anything on this subject without saying something that is true. What you must see is whether the truth shines through the words or whether they are platitudes, words repeated by rote. Look behind the words. Feel!'

I felt as might a man blind from birth suddenly ordered to see. I felt as inadequate as a donkey with two legs. He might as well have said 'Fly'.

That was the way he treated me, forcing me to see that it was not just a matter of his having a superior mind or of my not knowing the jargon, but that there was a range of perceptions of a different order which he had and I had not. And since he never pretended to be anything more than an ordinary man, I could not take refuge in the plea that he was extraordinary and that nothing could be expected of ordinary mortals like me. It was the other way round. He was asking me to be as normal as himself and share with him the

everyday elements of his experience. That was why I felt such a
fool: he was holding out something for me to take. He was holding
it, and I could not see what there was to take hold of.

A few evenings later I was sitting in his room. 'Look at the
psychic content of those books,' he said, waving towards the yellow-
painted pine shelves that filled one wall. I looked, and felt a familiar
numbness creeping over my brain that would reduce my contribu-
tion to monosyllables. 'See their inner content,' he continued, and
I knew he was not referring to the paper and print, nor even to the
information they contained. And he went on talking of symbols and
correspondences, planets and medicinal herbs, consciousness and
form, the levels of the universe, ghosts, dreams, *mahatmas*, ritual
gestures and their magical effects, and psychic phenomena, until the
very planks we sat on were surface appearances, bubbles of illusion
brought into being by the consciousness of the levels.

He would pile up conceptual images and set them glowing,
lighten philosophy with laughter, lead his audience to high seriousness, then drop to trivial gossip and, catching at a thread, draw
them up again. One cannot reproduce such talk, and little purpose
would be served if one could. On these occasions his purpose was
not to teach but to inspire. Many men can talk on a wide range of
subjects and hold an audience with a show of learning and wit;
university professors make a living out of it, as Krishna Prem once
said, living like yogis, on air . . . hot air. Krishna Prem's own
impassioned dedication to the spirit infused everything he said.
Visitors would leave him charged, not merely with this play of
original and interesting ideas but with some spark drawn from
Krishna Prem's own unshakable certainty. When, as sometimes
happened, a departed visitor would write, asking him to repeat his
talk on paper, Krishna Prem would smile ruefully; the point had
been missed. It was not what he said that mattered, but what came
through the words. If anyone grasped the certainty, nursing the
spark of inspiration, then, when occasion permitted, Krishna Prem
would turn to shorter and more practical instruction.

He never lectured in a monologue. The talks were conversational
meetings in which visitors were expected to participate. Contrived
questions were disposed of shortly, for he objected, he said, to being

treated like a model engine in a show-case where people put a coin in the slot to see the wheels go round. And if anyone produced a written list of questions or, worse still, paper and pencil to record the answers, he might refuse to talk at all. But when people came with personal questions and problems, he might give of himself until he was drained of energy. How much he gave depended on the particular case, for he seemed able to sense the integrity of the questioner, piercing the screen of words to try him with the touchstone of his heart. I am not suggesting that he was an omniscient superman with X-ray eyes. Like anyone learning his trade, he made mistakes, but there were few who could deceive him because he did not deceive himself.

This sort of insight was more than psychological skill, for men like Krishna Prem have added another dimension to their beings and they view others from that vantage point. Unlike a physician who tends to equate a man with his body, or a psychologist who equates a man with his mental–emotional complex, Krishna Prem equated a man with his spirit. Although such a statement passes the limits of most men's comprehension, it is the simple truth. The spiritual dimension is potentially present in all men, dormant, like a seed. Sometimes Krishna Prem would see a seed sprout, and the joy of that moment was recompense for all his years of effort.

Proselytizing was abhorrent to him. He did not want anyone to follow him or to join the particular sect to which he was outwardly affiliated. If he wanted anything, it was that people should get a feeling for the essential and non-denominational truth and grope their way towards it by any means that suited their particular characters and idiosyncrasies.

One difference between Moti and her mother was that where Yashoda Mai treated her favourites more gently than other disciples, Moti concentrated her wrath on those who were closest to her. 'Poor young man,' said Krishna Prem when he saw Moti beginning to take an interest in me. But it was also 'poor Sri Krishna Prem', for Moti devoted the last few years of her life to giving him the treatment her mother had spared him. It seems that her object was to smash the barriers of intellectual indifference which Krishna Prem habitually raised between himself and others as protection from painful involvement. She relied on his affection for her bearing the strain of the suffering she imposed on him. If it held, he would come to accept emotional pain as an essential part of life against which one must not erect barriers when one aspires to psychic wholeness. If one cannot accept it, one cannot transcend the *dwandas*, the opposites, for one is accepting only the gentle aspect of divinity and avoiding the harsh.

Krishna Prem emerged from the ordeal a softer, kinder and very much wiser man. The barriers were gone, so that people who knew him only in his later years remember him even more for the unrestricted warmth of his affection than for the brilliance of his expositions of the spiritual path. The brilliance remained, but it was more of the soft glow of a pearl, that pearl of great price, than the hard glitter of the diamond mind. As he says in the article entitled 'Symbolism and Knowledge', 'feeling and thought have to be fused into a unity'.

It was some ten years after Moti's death before that fusion was complete. Then, as if drawn by a magnet, visitors began to flood the little ashram. The man who had previously resented the least invasion of his privacy now opened his heart to these travellers on the dusty road of life, constantly giving of himself. He now embodied the truths he had previously so keenly perceived, so it was now the man and not simply the cogency and clarity of his thought that impressed people who met him. Previously he had given expression to the truth in a glittering parade of words, now it was as if the wordless truth shone through him, so that people often found as much teaching in his casual acts and gestures as they had done in his books.

During those intervening years he had learned to distinguish between the accessories to the religious path and the essentials which are not, in any ordinary sense, religious. He gradually abandoned the rigid framework of orthodox Hindu discipline which contained and guided his early growth. He simplified the temple ritual, retaining only those parts of the ceremonies that speak directly to the human soul. He disposed of the ashram library, keeping only such books as he felt would be of direct value to his disciples. And he radically altered his personal behaviour.

It was no easy task to break from a discipline which had ruled his actions for twenty-five years. But in face of what he had found, the detailed prescriptions of any orthodoxy were inessential trivialities. He saw no purpose in imposing them on a later generation of seekers whose social climate differed both from that of his upbringing and from that of his adoption. Both East and West were changing. People were seeking in a less mythological, more direct mode than the strictly religious approaches provided for. He constantly urged his hearers to pass beyond the study of theories and opinions and to press inwards to discover for themselves those realms of the spirit to which the different religions have given so many descriptions. Though he never claimed authority for what he said, his quiet confidence and the practicality of his advice were evidence enough that he knew the way because he had travelled it himself.

He neither gave himself the airs of a conventional guru nor assumed a false humility. He cooked, cleaned, and worked about the temple and garden as unaffectedly as the most ordinary of men. To the end he was intellectually active, studying Persian so as to read Jalal-ud-din Rumi in the original. Perhaps one of his most outstanding qualities showed itself in the way he could divest himself of authority, handing over the trusteeship of the ashram, the uncompleted manuscript of a book, responsibility for the temple management, even his personal correspondence and the initiation and instruction of his followers to a disciple who was thereby forced to overcome his reluctance to face any such challenges. With a show of petulance he would refuse to meet a group of visitors and send me to talk to them. I would reluctantly go, complaining that it would end by his having to see them as they would not be put off with a substitute. Then I would force myself to answer the standard questions with the standard answers while I dripped cold sweat from the effort to overcome my shyness and the visitors kept glancing in the direction from which they hoped Krishna Prem would appear. Then there was his unaffected pleasure when he walked in on one such session and the visitors, engrossed in talk, barely noticed his presence.

This was all part of his teaching, consonant with his goal of wholeness or perfection. Though he laid considerable stress on meditative practices, regarding them as the most essential part of the work, he held that the work is not complete until the whole from which all things have come is reflected in the wholeness of the man. A man under the sway of inhibitions and compulsions he regarded as partial or incomplete. If through fear one attempted to avoid certain areas of worldly experience, then, when one turned to meditation, the inner or psychic causes of that fear would rise up and bar one's progress. He therefore saw the work as a dialectical process: the facing of outer challenges opening the way to inner perception, and self-surrendering to the spirit in meditation giving rise to a trans-personal courage with which the challenges of life can be met. That self-surrender, he said, is the surrender of love, and the courage is the courage of love.

During the protracted and painful illness which led to his death in 1965, he continued guiding his disciples, constantly demonstrating in a manner more powerful than words the supremacy of the human spirit over the sufferings of the body.

The essays republished here were mostly written just before and during the first years of the Second World War. A few years before his death Sri Krishna Prem intended editing this selection for publication, but the increasing demands of disciples and visitors prevented his taking the work in hand. I have attempted to select portions which are and always should be applicable to the problems of human life, removing only those sections whose relevance was strictly contemporary. With the exception of the opening passage of 'Religion and Philosophy', which appeared in a small magazine around 1925, the essays appeared as editorials or articles in *The Review of Philosophy and Religion*, published in Allahabad, for which Krishna Prem held joint editorial responsibility with his friend Professor R. N. Kaul. Two of these essays formed the substance of a booklet twice printed in India as *Initiation into Yoga*. This was so well received that it is again included here.

Though these essays belong to Krishna Prem's earlier years and reflect his aspiration, rather than the certainty of attainment, he felt that they still adequately represented his basic attitudes.

SRI MADHAVA ASHISH

1. Initiation into Yoga

One of the greatest obstacles to the finding of Truth is the belief current among religious people that Truth is written down in some book or books which constitute the 'sacred scripture' for them. The orthodox Christians consider the Bible to be the inspired word of God in spite of its making a number of statements of fact which are quite certainly incorrect, and orthodox Hindus say that the Vedas are *apaurusheya*, which presumably means that they have no human authors, in spite of the fact that they are quite obviously the compositions of certain *rishis*. Similarly, every religion and sect has its holy books which are taken on trust without question although a great deal of ingenuity has to be expended upon attempts to make their statements square with knowledge derived from other sources.

It is by no means intended here to depreciate those ancient writings, some of which are among the most inspiring productions of the human mind and contain realizations and intuitions which are of great help to a seeker, but it cannot be too strongly emphasized that an attitude of blind acceptance of what is written in any book is definitely harmful and effectually serves to prevent the attainment of Truth.

It is sometimes argued that even if the books in question were not written by God (whatever that may mean) they were the work of great Seers whose knowledge was far greater than ours and so should be accepted on trust. But this too will not do.

In the first place we do not know who did actually write the books. It may have been the Seer himself or it may have been one of his disciples with an only partial understanding of his master's teaching. It may even have been made up by some one who wished to gain a hearing for his ideas by fathering them on to a great name. It is for instance preposterous to suppose that Vyāsa, the Hindu Sage, wrote all that appears nowadays in his name, the whole set of

Purāṇas and Epics with all their mutual contradictions which not all the ingenuity of a Benares pundit can reconcile satisfactorily.

In the second place we know for a fact that, during the transmission of the books through all the centuries that separate us from their authors, all sorts of corruptions have crept into the texts. Important passages have been dropped out and new passages have been inserted.

In the third place, even if we assume that in the book in question we have the exact words of the original Seer who wrote it, it is still not desirable that we should accept it blindly. The words of the book are not the Truth he saw but the verbal expression of it that he judged suitable for the time and place. Every day we see that words mean different things to different persons and it is absurdly optimistic to suppose that the words addressed to disciples two thousand years ago will convey the same meaning to us today.

Moreover, the idea that a statement in a book can constitute knowledge is an utter absurdity. The books contain a number of black marks on white paper (or the equivalent), and what these marks signify to us depends upon the ideas in our own minds, and they in turn upon the experiences we have gone through. Without having lived through the appropriate experience, it is quite impossible for us to understand in any real sense the meaning of what is written in any book, no matter who the author may have been.

I repeat, however, that it is not intended to depreciate the study of the ancient scriptures. I, for one, have derived great benefit from such study and would be the last person to wish for a general bonfire of scriptures. What is wanted, however, is not blind belief but intelligent study. Belief, as the word is usually understood, is an irrelevance, a futility and a hindrance. The mind is the mirror of the universe. If that mirror is kept clean and not distorted, it gives a picture of the world which, though, as it were, a two dimensional rendering of a three dimensional reality, is yet a perfectly true one. The mind works perfectly upon its own level. It is a wondrous mirror extending throughout the universe, but, if its bright images are to correspond with the facts, it is essential that it should not be distorted in any way. The great distorting forces are hopes and fears or, as we may put it in another way, it is desire, whether positive or negative.

When a man says he believes in something or other (I do not mean rational belief based on consideration of evidence) it would be more correct to say that he hopes that it may be true and, action and reaction being equal and opposite, he at the same time fears that it is not. Every belief then has its corresponding doubt lurking somewhere in the shadow. It is for this reason that men of strong religious beliefs become so fanatical. Silently gnawing at their hearts, insidiously whispering in their ears, is an army of doubts, shadowy beings inhabiting a twilight world but corresponding exactly with the beliefs which, like so many children's kites, go soaring up into the bright sunshine. It is to silence those whispers, to lay those ghosts in the basement, that the believer strives with all his might to convert others to his creed. Criticism he cannot stand because of the echoes that it raises down below where all should be silence; and so, just in proportion as he increases the force of his own beliefs, he magnifies the tension within and, filled with an inner hatred of himself, he vents his explosive anger upon others. Thus from a mere fanatic he becomes a persecutor.

What, then, should be our attitude towards the ancient scriptures, or, indeed, towards books in general? Books may be divided into two classes: those that are based upon inner experience and those that are mere words strung together with more or less skill. The latter class may be ignored altogether. It may be asked: how, if we are ourselves ignorant, we may know that a book is based upon genuine experience? The answer is that the Truth exists already in our hearts, however ignorant our outer personalities may be; it is a sheer fact that words that spring from deep realization raise echoes within us if we listen to them with free minds. The words, as we say, mean something to us. Perhaps there may be other books, equally the fruit of some one's experience, which raise no echoes within. In that case it is some lack of sympathy or of experience, some knot of prejudice in our minds, that prevents our hearts from acting as resonators, and so we put the book aside. When that happens it is doubtless a pity but it cannot be helped; we are not ready for that particular message and its study can do us no good.

B

If, however, a book does 'mean something to us', if we have reason, inner reason, to think that it is a record of actual experience, we should set aside all questions of its date and authorship, its orthodoxy or heterodoxy, its agreement or disagreement with other books. Instead, we should give our hearts to its study, trying to penetrate behind the words to the thoughts and realization for the expression of which those words were selected.

An instance may make it clearer. Shankarāchārya, as is well known, affirmed that everything is the Self (*Ātmā*), while the Buddha proclaimed as the essence of wisdom the perception of the not-Self nature (*nairātmya*) of reality. The average reader has either already taken sides upon the subject and so treats one of the views as simply wrong, or else considers it a matter for argument and debates it with himself or with others, hoping thereby to arrive at the Truth. But this is quite the wrong procedure. We must remember that reality is not labelled so that a man who has seen it has merely to read the label correctly and all is well. Reality is beyond the mind and its labels. We affix them for our own convenience, but it is we who made them, and they are never more than symbolic finger posts pointing the way to what is beyond. Moreover, they are symbols that mean different things to different persons.

Instead, therefore, of assuming Self (*ātmā*) and not-Self (*anātmā*) are things of which one is true and the other false, we must remember that they are attempted descriptions in words of some characteristic of what was experienced without words. Instead of asking which is the true description, we should try and understand what characteristic it was of the experienced reality that led Shankara to use just the term he did, and what the characteristic which led the Buddha to use its apparent opposite. We shall then find there is no contradiction, for in fact they were not talking of the same characteristics at all.

I have said so much about books because, nowadays at least, books form the usual starting point of the search, and it is important that in using them we should use them correctly and not incorrectly for, in the latter case, we shall merely fill our heads with empty notions. The Truth is within us, and books are only useful in so far as they crystallize and make manifest what is, till then, only obscurely known. Such a statement as 'God created the world' is, for instance, entirely meaningless unless we have at least some idea of what we mean by 'God' and what by 'created'. It is hardly necessary to say that, for most people who use the phrase so glibly, the words in question have practically no meaning whatever. If such a person is asked about the origin of the world he will reply 'God created it' and then, if asked what he means by God, he will say that God is the creator of the world. This sounds almost too absurd to be true but is nevertheless a very common reply and may serve as typical of a great many 'explanations' which are completely circular.

It is time now to pass from the subject of books to that of a teacher or guru. There is a current belief in India that it is impossible to make any progress on the spiritual path without the help of a guru. As a result of this belief all sorts of mistakes are made. One type of person promptly gets himself initiated by the family guru who may be anything from a competent professional ritualist to an ignorant mouther of formulated humbug. Another type goes to a famous guru in one of the great pilgrimage centres such as Benares, Brindaban or Ayodhya, and, for a suitable fee, gets himself enrolled among the army of the great man's followers. A third, not unreasonably dissatisfied with the observed results in the two former cases, wanders about in search of *sādhūs*, of whom he usually sees so many that he finds himself unable to stick to any one in particular and wanders on hoping ever for the one unique *mahātma* who, with a wave of his hand, will send the disciple's '*kundalini*' spouting up like a fountain.

Now it is simply untrue that a man cannot make progress – even great progress – upon the Path without the help of an outer guru, and though it is undoubtedly a help to have a suitable guru, it is certain that for most of us there is much that can be done, much that *must* be done by our own unaided efforts before the presence of an outer guru is necessary or even useful. This will become clearer when we have seen who or what the true Guru really is.

The Guru is the pure Consciousness itself dwelling in the heart of every living being and particularly that Light as reflected in the *sāttvic buddhi* – the power that gives us certain knowledge beyond all the doubts and hesitations of the mind. That Light dwells in all

beings and speaks (that is why some traditions have termed it the
Logos, the Word) in our hearts with the voice of conscience;
though only too often we confuse its voice with various other
voices that speak with louder accents. At this point the reader
usually smiles his acquaintance with various learned theories about
race heredity, parental influence and Freudian super-egos. I am not
concerned here to enter into these bye-paths, some of which are
quite interesting to explore. In spite of them all, however, it is a sheer
fact that there is a Light within us which knows the truth; a Voice
which commands the right with absolute certainty. I am quite
aware of the many volumes that have been written in criticism of
such views. Views are matters of words, well- or ill-chosen, and so
are liable to criticism, well- or ill-founded. Facts, the facts which
views are intended to explain, are quite another thing; they are
not open to criticism. Whatever may be said in criticism of the
above will be criticism of the words with which I have expressed it.
The fact is there – state it how you please.

That is why Shiva, the *Ātman* or Universal Self, is said to be the
jagadguru, the Teacher of the world, and that, too, is why it is said
that the Guru is the same as God, a true statement which has enabled
a lot of rascally humbugs to get themselves paid divine honours by
their dupes. The Guru is the same as God because the Guru is God,
the *antaryāmi* or Inner Ruler, dwelling in the heart. There is no need
to wander from place to place, visiting sacred pilgrimage centres or
crag-perched monasteries in Tibet, in order to find the Guru. Quite
literally he is there within us, but though his silent voice is constantly
teaching us, we usually do not listen, and it is for this reason that an
outer guru is a help upon the Path.

The outer Guru is one who has so far identified himself with the
Self which is in all that he is able to speak with its voice. Not because
of great learning, great asceticism, or great supernatural powers
should a man be chosen as the outer Guru, but because his words
penetrate to the heart and raise echoes there within its caves. To the
inner Guru we can, and too often do, turn a deaf ear. We prefer to
listen to the voices of desire, of the senses and of prejudice, and so
hear nothing of the Soundless Voice within. The voice of the outer
Guru, on the other hand, is at least certain to penetrate to our ears.

He too will not compel (for no true guru will trespass upon the free-will of his disciple) but at least he will put the truth fairly before us so that, if we refuse assent, it will be with full knowledge of what we are doing. Like Sri Krishna in the Gita, he will say to us, 'having reflected over this fully, do as thou wishest'. It is for us to recognize the truth of his words, to resolve to practise them and to put forth the necessary effort. But men are fundamentally lazy. We want someone to do everything for us, to transform us into yogis without our having to go through the long and painful struggles that are necessary. Consequently, we are only too apt to feel that if a guru cannot do that for us it is he and not we who are to blame.

As stated above, the Guru can only teach us the Path; he cannot force us to tread it. And, therefore, before the teachings of a Guru can be of any use to us, we must have learnt at least some degree of control over our unruly desires and senses; otherwise his words will be useless to us for we shall not practise them. Moreover we shall not be able even to recognize the Guru until we have formed the habit of listening to the Inner Voice, since we shall not be able to know that the two voices are in agreement.

If, however, we will bend our efforts towards controlling the senses by the mind and to listening in the mind for the Voice which comes from beyond, it is perfectly certain that, as soon as an outer Guru is necessary, that Guru will be found. As an ancient saying has it 'when the disciple is ready, the Guru appears'.

But it will not do merely to wait passively for him to appear. The aspirant must make himself ready and practise a strenuous self-discipline both of his actions and of his thoughts. Above all, of his thoughts, for, as the *Dhammapada* puts it, 'Of all things thought is the forerunner and the chief element; all things are thought'. If the thoughts are controlled, the actions will follow, but, if the mind is like a riderless horse, no amount of austere discipline in the realm of action will be of use.

Control of the mind, however, does not here mean the ability to hold it vacant of all thought – that is something that will be dealt with in its proper place – but the subjecting of the mind to the rule of what is inwardly felt to be right, or, as the Gita puts it, the replacement of motivation based on attraction and repulsion (*rāga* and *dwesha*) by one based on the idea of duty or rightness (*swadharma*). This is the all important *karma yoga* dealt with in the second chapter of the Gita and it must be practised before the aspirant is ready for anything else. The mind is the gateway which leads to the know-ledge of the Reality, and it must be thoroughly cleansed of the thorns and thickets of desire before it can turn on its hinges and allow the traveller a sight of the wonderful world beyond.

It has been said before that the mind is like a marvellous mirror extending through the universe. Unfortunately, it is usually turned only towards the senses and so reflects only the illusory appearance of the world. Never mind the vexed question as to whether the world is an illusion or not; like most such problems it is a question of words rather than of facts. The fact is that the world of common-sense experience, the world of solid material objects, of separate individual selves, is not the true world, call it what you please. There are no solid material objects; there are no separate individual selves. All that is illusion, illusion seated in the senses or rather in that aspect of the mind that unites with them. Even physicists are nowadays coming to see that it is the mind that creates the world of so-called physical objects. Philosophers – even in the West – have seen it long ago, and though the words in which they expressed their insight were usually, if not always, inadequate and so liable to hostile criticism, yet it must be always borne in mind by the truth-seeker that insight does not stand or fall by the words in which it is ex-pressed. This is one of the most important things for us to learn. The finger must never be confused with the moon it points to. This is one of the reasons for the contradictory language so often used by mystics. They know that grasp of words will never give grasp of truth, and so by contradictions and paradoxes they attempt to force such seekers as are educable at all out of their grip on words. They behave, in fact, like birds who push their young ones out of the nest so forcing them to use their wings and exchange the limitations of the nest for the vast freedom of the living air.

To return however to the mind: it is the outflowing of desire that creates the world of selves and objects. The Buddha and other eastern Seers taught long ago that desire is the creator of the world, and now philosophers and psychologists in their slow way are coming to see it too. Kant taught that we never know things-in-themselves (as he termed the reality) since all our knowledge is moulded by the categories of the mind. William James taught that truth is purely pragmatic, that the mind accepted things as true because they worked in practice or, in other words, because they satisfied desires. Bergson, too, showed how the intellect was at the service of practical needs (desire again) and added that reality itself was only to be known by intuitions, while Freud, Jung, and other psychologists are never tired of stressing how the workings of the mind are controlled by the surges of desire in what they term 'the unconscious'.

Yet in practice all these thinkers have remained bound to the notion of an external world of inert objects. Their thought has lacked courage. However much they taught that things were thought, they have remained fettered by them. Not one of them has been able to mould those waves of thought that ordinary men call things. And yet this can be done. This solid world can 'melt, thaw and resolve itself into a dew', before our very eyes, though, if any man should come along who can cause even a pin's head to vanish, philosophers and thinkers lose their heads and begin to prattle foolishly of gods and miracles. They have not had the courage to follow the seers and mystics who have taught and shown that the mind must first be withdrawn from the false shadow show that it mistakes for the sunlight of life, withdrawn into an inner belt of darkness which some have termed the mystic death, others the dark night of the soul, before its mirror is turned round to face reality and reflect the Sun of Truth shining beyond the darkness.

Nothing in the unplumbed depths of the universe is too far away in space, nothing in all the countless millions of years of time is too remote for us to know it here and now. Even the trivialities of crystal gazing show how space and time are no bars to the mirror of the mind of which the actual crystal or what-not is but a symbol, a wretched concession to our faith in outward things. The real yogi needs no crystal, no pool of ink to help him see. He has only to direct his mind to that which he wishes to know and it is there in front of him.

But it is not such knowledge that the yogi seeks. Knowledge of forms, however remote in time or space, is but a knowledge of illusions. Far beyond all forms, shining for ever in the light of an eternal summer, lies the Realm of Truth. None can describe that Realm, though gleams of its splendour have gilded the words of poets and thinkers so that they tell us fitfully of a beauty beyond all words, a beauty which is the same as Truth.

To reach that Truth the inner path must be trodden. The mind, first purified by the practice of right action, must learn to check all its movements and to allow its flame to burn steadily like a lamp in a place where the winds of desire no longer blow. It is no use trying to hold it still by sheer force, no more use than it would be to try and fix the flame of a lamp by a pair of pliers. The yogi must study its workings and gain insight into the currents of desire that cause trains of thought to spring up and pursue their endless linked processions in our hearts. It is not force, the so-called force of concentration, but calm insight and detachment that will bring about the cessation of the streaming phantoms, and it is only when they have ceased that the mind 'stands in its own nature', as Patanjali puts it, and is ready to reverse itself and plunge into the cool and life giving waters of the Realm of Truth.

Thus the mind goes beyond itself. The drop merges within the shining Sea of Light; yet, since the whole is mirrored in the drop, the drop itself becomes the Sea, no longer self but All.

In the preceding pages it has been urged that there does actually exist a Path the treading of which leads to full knowledge of the Truth. It is a Path that has existed in all ages and in all countries, though the names by which it was known have differed widely. The Quest of the Holy Grail, the Search for the Elixir of Life or the Philosopher's Stone, the *Devayāna* or Pathway of the Gods are all terms for the same Path, the knowledge of which has always existed and may be found hidden beneath the symbols of sacred books, carved in stone in ancient monuments, cunningly concealed in the apparent phantasies of alchemists and echoing feebly in the rituals of Masonic lodges.

In some lands it has been forced underground by the embattled powers of established churches and forced to disguise itself in intentionally obscure allegories; while, in others, it was found that, by setting it up on a pedestal for worship as something too holy to be trodden by anyone except the great saints of a distant past, it could be removed from the sphere of real life and the urgency of its message conveniently dimmed. Our present age of enlightenment has discovered the easiest method of all. No longer need it be either suppressed or worshipped: it can be 'explained!'

However, in spite of the inquisitions, the temples and the learned Sciences of Comparative Nonsense, the Knowledge still exists, the Path which leads to it exists, and those who tread that Path exist and form a brotherhood, even when unknown to each other, perhaps the only true brotherhood in a world maddened by hatred, greed and stupidity.

Although this Path is the hidden basis of all religions it has but little connection with any religion as such. This is clearly shown by the way in which its teachers were always rejected by the leaders of institutional religion. To name only a few, the Buddha was an unbeliever (*nāstika*), Christ a blasphemer, Shankara a disguised Buddhist, Socrates a corrupter of youth, Eckhart a heretic and St Germain a charlatan! Such at least were the verdicts of their orthodox contemporaries. Only when the sharp edge of the Teaching had been blunted by human stupidity, when use and want had enabled men to throw over the shoulders of the departed Teacher the cloak of a deific respectability, only then was it possible for the mass of men to build their churches and temples to the Teacher, to domesticate the Divine Fire in harmless household lanterns and to replace the fiery Wine of Spirit with the lemonade of conventional piety.

In the pages that follow the term Yoga has been used as a synonym for this Path, but if anyone should dispute the appropriateness of the usage on the ground that it does not agree with the teachings of his favourite book on the subject he is requested to throw this paper on the fire and return forthwith to his books.

Lastly, it should be plainly stated that, although this Path is that of the alchemists who transmute base metal into gold, it is useless to expect it to contain any simple psychic tricks by which hatred may be transmuted into love, greed into non-attachment and stupidity into wisdom. These transmutations can be, must be and will be accomplished, but there is no easy, effortless or mechanical way of achieving them. The Path is one to be followed through many lives, and none of us are likely to go far upon it unless we care for it more, infinitely more, than we do for anything else in this or any world.

In the few pages that follow only the first steps are set forth, yet most of us will find their treading hard enough. Apologies are offered to the reader for the imperfections which assuredly do not belong to that on which it is based.

The word yoga as used here signifies the method by which man can unite his finite self with Infinite Being. Those whose interest lies in scholarly discussions about Patanjali's *Yoga Sūtras* or other classical text-books of yoga will find nothing in it to interest them. The line of approach here set forth is not based upon any of the classical authorities and, indeed, makes no appeal to any authority save whatever may be found in itself.

The path of yoga is an inner path, and too much concern with what others have said or written, especially when those books were written centuries or millennia ago, is apt to be more of a hindrance than a help. It is true that the great masters of yoga all over the world have, in their different ways, all said very much the same thing, but it is also true that they have, for the most part, said it in languages that are no longer current and in words which have changed their meanings during the passing centuries. Though much of a general nature may undoubtedly be learnt from the study of the books, yet too much attention to them is apt to degenerate into mere theorizing about the meanings of the words instead of trying to find out by actual experience what the facts really are. When it comes to real practice we must drop the books, useful as they have been in giving a general direction to our aim, and adventure for ourselves along the pathway whose gate is in our hearts.

The first thing to be considered before setting out on that journey is its motive. The motives which impel man to the practice of yoga may be divided into three. The first is the desire to escape from the burdens of life. Such a motive, however, though it is generally thought to have the sanction of famous names, is very definitely an inferior one, for it is based on fear, and everyone knows that fear is a weakening emotion. In this quest all the strength of the soul is needed, for, as the Upanishad says, 'not by the weak is this *Ātman* to be attained'. Courage is one of the necessary qualifications of the aspirant and it cannot grow in the soil of a timid flight from the stresses and strains of worldly life.

A second motive is the desire for psychic powers and strange experiences. This, too, will not lead to the true goal, for, though it has not the weakening effect of fear, it is rooted in self and so strengthens the ego, the very thing that yoga aims at utterly transcending.

The third and only satisfactory motive is the love of the Eternal, the aspiration towards that white radiance which, dimly sensed through the many-coloured symbols of the Gods, is yet 'the fountain light of all our day'. Fear may cause us to shrink back, turtle-like, from the contacts of life; curiosity may expand our selves into the remotest corners of the manifested universe; but only with the wings of an ardent love can we soar upon the Swan's Path to the Sun beyond the Darkness.

The love which is here referred to is, however, not a love for the purely transcendent Eternal alone but for that Eternal as manifested in the universe. Quite early on the path the aspirant comes to see, if only dimly, that the one Eternal is within the hearts of all that live, within even those things that we call dead. Therefore, he who seeks to tread the way of self-transcendence must cease to think of any proud and exclusive treading of the path for his own self alone. There have been those who have made of their knowledge a barrier between themselves and their fellow men. This path is one which all will some day tread, few though there be at any given moment. Therefore the aspirant must seek to share such knowledge as he has with his fellows or else he will build up barriers of illusion around himself, the great illusion of separateness that Buddhist writers condemn so emphatically. All life is one, and he who wishes to save his own soul shall lose it.

So much for the motivation of the quest: we have now to consider the means to be employed. The cause of bondage lies in the mind, for, as we read in *Maitri Upanishad*: 'The world is verily the mind; therefore the latter should be purified with all effort. As a man's mind is, so he becomes; this is the eternal secret.'

It is the truth that the origin of the world is in the mind, though this does not mean, as certain naïve subjectivists have held, that the world is inside our heads, for heads and brains are themselves parts of the world. That mind which originates and embraces the world must, if considered as localized in space at all, be thought of as extending beyond the farthest confines of the starry universe. Within that mind, through the agency of what the *Yogāchāra* school of Buddhists termed constructive ideation or, better, constructive imagination (*abhūtaparikalpa*), the whole world of objects floats in the void, like clouds in a summer sky, or, to quote the ancient simile, like the towered city of the Gandharvas seen in the sunset clouds. It is by the mind that the whole mass of suffering that we call the world has been evolved, and it is in the mind that the dread spectre must be exorcized so that in its stead the vision of harmonious Reality may dawn.

The web of fate has been woven in our own minds and it is there that it must be rent if we are to stand in our own true nature and cease to be what Hermes termed mere processions of Fate. But it is not by any sudden wrench that the task can be accomplished; rather, the woven tissue must be unpicked thread by thread. Therefore the first task that faces us in the attempt to master this Demiurgos, this world-maker, is to train ourselves to think clearly, to turn the light of clear consciousness upon the very thought processes themselves as they twine and untwine, weaving the web of the world.

With most people thought is but the servant of desire. Thoughts come and go obeying, not their own laws, but those of the sub-mental desire nature. In order to see this, one has only to practise for a little the Freudian analytic technique of allowing free associations to come into one's mind. Unerringly the thoughts sink lower and lower till they become unblushingly sexual, and it is on this fact that the pan-sexualism of Freud's theories is based.

But it is not necessary that thought should be the slave of desire in this manner. If it is trained to follow its proper laws, the laws inherent in its own higher nature, it is capable of revealing the truth (at least upon its own plane, for there is that which is still higher) and of becoming the rudder of the soul, enabling the latter to cleave a passage through the waters of desire, regardless of their

hostile currents. Therefore it is taught that we should live a life full
of thought so that by degrees the mind may learn to be the master
in its own house.

For this to happen, though, it is necessary for the thought to be
always clear. An unclear thought can no more be a safe guide than
a crooked line can be said to point in any particular direction. We
must above all check the tendency to allow vague and woolly
thoughts to pursue one another in our minds like so many sheep.
Such confused thinking is quite useless. Each thought must stand
out clearly like an object seen in bright sunshine, for only then will
it be able to resist the fatal downward pull and to escape the mon-
sters of desire which are ever waiting with open mouths to drag it
into the depths below.

At the same time care must be taken to guard against an egoistic
pride, the besetting vice of the ordinary intellectual, who is only too
prone to fancy himself a being apart and to look down on those
struggling beneath him with a tolerant contempt saying, perhaps,

> There is no better way
> Than patient scorn, nor any help for man,
> Nor any staying of his whirling wheel.

The aspirant must therefore guard himself carefully against any
tendency to separate himself from his fellows. This he can do only
by an effort of imaginative sympathy. He must strive always to feel
himself into the hearts of those he meets in his daily life, to see things
from their point of view, to feel the impacts of events and particularly the impact of his own actions as they would feel them. In this
way he will learn to understand instead of blaming his fellow men,
and will learn also that his enemies are not the villains that he
previously supposed them to be but merely rather foolish people,
prone to deceive themselves about their motives as is he himself.

Training himself in this way, the aspirant gradually breaks down
the barriers which separate him from his fellow beings and will
acquire the power of thinking and acting in an unegotistic manner,
for he will no longer concern himself solely with his own point of
view. His actions will become those which are best for all concerned
and so his body will become an instrument for the fulfilment, not

of his own selfish desires, but of the needs of all. That which embraces all will act through him, though those for whom he acts may know it not.

It is time now to return to the mind and its thought processes, for, as the Upanishad quoted above goes on to say, 'it is the mind that is the cause of the bondage or liberation of men'. By listening to the voices of desire the mind has led us into all this suffering. Its winged freedom has been lost by stooping to the lure of the senses and its feet have become entangled in the sticky lime. This being so, some have thought to free it by a forcible asceticism, and torture the body in the hope of freeing the soul. This self torture may take many forms, from the crudely sensational fastings and beds of spikes to the more subtle puritanism which treats all bodily joys as something evil to be avoided.

All such self-torture, whether crude or refined, is a mistake. The mind is not, on this plane of existence, something entirely separate from the body. As the poet-seer William Blake wrote: 'Man has no Body distinct from his Soul, for that called Body is a portion of Soul discerned by the five Senses, the chief inlets of Soul in this age.'

It is true that, by weakening the body, visions and psychic experiences may result; but it is also true that those visions are deceitful mirages which have misled many, for the tormented body reacts upon the mind and warps its vision so that it mistakes the distorted images of its own desires for truth. Many of the grotesque and fanatical cults that have arisen in the world owe their being to this very cause, and many a genuine mystic has lost himself among self-created illusions.

The best means of freeing the mind is not by weakening the body but by strengthening the mind itself by constant exercise. Whatever is not clear, whatever puzzles one in life, should be meditated upon constantly until the answer comes. It may take a long time, especially at first, but if the meditation is persisted in it is sure to come in the end. It is necessary, however, to be sure that the problem is clearly set before the mind and that its terms are clearly understood. There can be no answer to a question which, through lack of clarity in its terms, is really meaningless. If, however, the question is clearly framed and the meditation is persisted in untiringly, the solution is sure to be found, and what is more important still, the mind will be strengthened in the process. If, on the other hand, the attempt is given up because of its difficulty and the subject is allowed to sink back into the limbo of unsolved problems, the mind will be correspondingly weakened.

This strengthening and perfecting of the mind is of the utmost importance because it is the mind which is the gateway to the real Consciousness, and, as it is said in the *Kathopanishad*, 'by the mind is it (the *Ātman*) to be attained.' This may sound strange to some who have always considered that yoga is the cessation of mental processes and to others who have read that 'the mind is the great slayer of the Real'. But the mind has two aspects, a higher and a lower, according as to whether it is united with desire or free from it (see *Maitri Upanishad* 6.34) and it is the lower aspect enslaved to desire, that is the slayer of the Real. As for the cessation of mental processes, it is a sheer fact that such cessation is only possible when the aspirant is able to withdraw his consciousness through the mental door into the higher level beyond. Poised serenely on that higher level it is true that the mental flux will subside and cease, but all who have tried to reduce the mind to stillness will be aware of their failure to accomplish it except from that higher level.

The first step in fact is to find out the mind. While everyone talks glibly of his mind and his thoughts, yet it is a fact that most of what passes for thinking is mere verbal habit (as the Behaviourists would say), mere fragments of visual and other imagery floating on the tides of desire. Though all consider they possess minds, there are few who really know what it is they mean by the statement, and therefore the first step consists in finding out by introspection what it is that we really mean by the mind. It is not necessary to be able to give a definition of it but it is essential that the seeker should be able to recognize it for himself, to separate it out, as it were, and to know in his own experience what it really is whether he can describe it adequately in words or not.

Having found out the mind, found it in the sense in which one finds and recognizes the colour red, indefinable though the latter may be, the next step is to detach oneself from it. One should ask oneself the question: 'whose is this mind and what is the "I" who has found out and is contemplating it?' Once more, a verbal answer is utterly useless. One must be able to view the mind as something quite separate and distinct, and then turn round, as it were, and see what actually is the viewer of the mind. It is not intended to give the answer here both because the essential part of the whole process is that we should find the answer for ourselves and because whatever verbal description might be given would mean quite different things to different readers. It must be seen by and for oneself.

Having detached oneself from the mind, the next step is to watch calmly the flux of thoughts as they come and go, to observe them with the same impartial objectivity with which one would observe a stream of passers-by outside one's window. The aspirant must carefully observe how the thought stream coheres together and what are its laws. Just as he would observe that in the street a band (of a certain recognizable sort) is nearly always followed by soldiers, and a dead body by a procession of mourners, so he must observe that certain states of mind, which he must learn to recognize, are always followed by certain other ones, beneficial or harmful.

For instance, there is a certain mood of depression, a certain sense of the fatality of all that happens and of the uselessness of all struggle which sometimes masquerades as a 'spiritual' state of submission to the will of God, of helplessness in the Divine hands, or some similar phrase. This state, however, differs from that of which it is a *tāmasik* parody by the fact that the following thought stream is always lowered in quality, that its succeeding states of mind are recognizably weakening and inferior. This is merely an instance to show the way in which it is necessary to follow up the consequences of one's mental states until they are all known and can be recognized as harmful or beneficial. It may be added that the practice is not simply one for certain hours of 'meditation' but one which must be kept up at all times. It may also be observed in passing that this is the process that underlies all those classifications and analyses of mental states which, in a rather tiresomely scholastic form, occupy a large part of Buddhist *abhidharma* literature. But no book knowledge will avail. Each must know his own mental states by direct awareness for himself. It may also be added that, if any reader is confident that he knows them already without any further practice, let him read a little of analytic psychology and he will very soon come to realize, probably with considerable horror, how very little he knows of what goes on within his mind.

Having observed the varying results of the different thoughts and feelings that flow through the mind, the next step, an obvious one, is to bend one's energies to the task of guiding them. Mental states which are now known to have harmful effects must be nipped in the bud before those effects have time to manifest, and the easiest method of doing this is that of deliberately invoking their opposite states. Thoughts, on the other hand, which have been seen to be beneficial should be encouraged. Once more it must be emphasized that this is an individual process. No set of rules in books, no hard and fast ethical codes are adequate to replace living personal experience. There must be complete freedom from conventional ethical prepossessions if this practice is not to lapse into sterility.

One habit in particular must be carefully checked and that is the habit of allowing the mind to run on aimlessly from one thing to another, of letting it take sudden flights from one subject to another and then back to the first without any control at all. Such a habit of mind is fatal for yoga, for it is the way of the mind when being led by desire, from which leading-strings it is the object of yoga to free it. Deep and dark run those mainly unconscious currents, and when the mind is jumping about or drifting aimlessly it is always a sign that their sinister guidance is in operation and should be checked. Whatever one is thinking about should form the sole object of the mental processes, and, as said before, however many times it may be necessary to come back, the effort to understand should not be abandoned till the problem becomes quite clear. Incidentally, the way to deal with a jumping or drifting mind is to stand back from it and observe where it is drifting to and why. Once that is found out, it will usually be relatively easy to bring it into control once more; mere attempts to hold it steady by force are not likely to be very successful. As in the Japanese art of Jiu-Jitsu, not brute strength, but skill is what is required.

The next topic that must be discussed is one which has already been dealt with on a previous page but which, on account of its importance as well as for the sake of completeness, must be touched on again. Whenever the mind is faced by two alternatives there is always present an intuition, even if it be but the dimmest sort of 'feeling', that one of the ways is right and the other wrong, or, at least, that one of them is better than the other and that, as the *Kathopanishad* puts it, the better (*śreya*) is one thing and the pleasant (*preya*) is another.

This intuition is always present, though, if not cultivated, it remains dim and we can easily blind ourselves to its presence. Nevertheless it is of the utmost importance, for it is the key to the door which leads from the lower mind to the higher and beyond. It must therefore, be carefully cultivated and strengthened by paying attention to and following it. Just as the trained ear of the engineer recognizes even a small 'knock' in his engines when nothing is perceptible to the ordinary untrained ear, so the aspirant must be always ready to listen for that subtle inner voice and, having heard it, he must always obey and allow the intuition to guide his other mental processes. Only in this way can he rise to a constant functioning in his higher mind. The path is extremely difficult and it is no wonder that many psychologists throw up their hands and proclaim that the mind is inevitably and permanently the slave of desire. But there is a way out of that slough of despond, and constant meditation along the above lines is the best way of treading it.

We now come to the problem of the control of the senses, a subject which many consider should be taken up at the very commencement. In the classical statement of the four qualifications, however, *dama* or control of the senses follows and not precedes *sama* or control of mind. The senses are the offspring of the mind, as the *Sānkhya* philosophy taught long ago. They are the *indriyas* of which the mind is *Indra* or the chief. To attempt to control the senses before the mind is in control is like trying to bale the water out of a leaky ship without first stopping the leak.

At this stage, however, they too must be brought under control, and this is done by keeping them under the guidance of a mind which is itself controlled by the inner voice referred to above. This is also the method recommended in the *Kathopanishad*, where, having compared the body to a chariot, the senses to the horses, the mind to the reins and the *buddhi* (the inner intuition, the faculty giving certain knowledge of right and wrong) to the charioteer, it goes on to say: 'He who is possessed of *buddhi*, whose mind always firmly adheres [to that *buddhi*], his senses are under control like the good horses of a chariot driver.'

It will thus be seen that the often advocated plan of attempting to control the senses first and then passing on to the mind is not only contrary to Upanishadic teaching but is also contrary to the facts. Without control of the mind, sense control is an impossibility, but, once the mind is trained to follow the inner voice, it becomes relatively easy.

The senses should not be allowed to work at their own will in a random manner. Whatever is experienced through or by the senses should have a definite purpose, and that purpose should be clearly focussed in thought before they are allowed to work. Later on the yogi will be able to withdraw his consciousness from his senses at will, leaving them perfectly inactive, but in these initial stages the aspirant will find that difficult, if not impossible, and he may content himself with allowing them to act under the discipline of the mind.

Above all, he should not try to kill out his senses by harsh treatment of them or by a forced inactivity. A wise moderation and not mortifying asceticism is what is needed. The latter has most disastrous results, for while the outer senses are being deadened by torture, the inner senses, those that are manifest in dream or phantasy, run riot and destroy all peace within the mind. That is why ascetics of the type of the famous St Anthony are always subject to illusions of being persecuted and tempted horribly by devils. Asceticism is not yoga, and never does one see in the eyes of the typical ascetic that calm poise and inner serenity that is the mark of the true yogi. It should never be forgotten that the inner senses (which are connected with what some modern psychologists term the unconscious) will take a frightful revenge for any forcible suppression of their outer brothers. Neurosis will certainly and even insanity may easily follow any such misguided attempts. Certainly no inner peace can be attained by such methods.

Instead of an outward suppression the aspirant should try to understand why it is that the senses desire to function in a particular manner. Directing his controlled mind upon their workings, he should calmly observe whether particular activities are followed by good results or bad, allowing the former quite freely, undeterred by the thought that the pleasure resulting is a 'sensuous' one, and checking the latter by the power of his mind. In this as in other matters he will do well to follow the wise practice of the Buddha:

When in following after happiness or after sense objects I have perceived that bad qualities developed and good qualities were diminished, then I have considered that that happiness or those sense objects are to be avoided while, when I have seen that the reverse is true, I have considered them fit to be followed after. (*Dīgha Nikāya* 21, somewhat abridged.)

At the same time, the mind itself must not be allowed to be invaded and captured by sensuous thoughts. The untrained mind is only too willing to allow itself to be mastered by the swarming phantasies which surge up from the desire nature, but the disciplined mind, knowing that that is the downward path and leads to danger, will carefully avoid such a state, and, however active the inner or outer senses may be allowed to be, will maintain its own watchfulness, calm and untouched by the sense life below.

One other warning may be added. The aspirant should never run away in fright from anything he finds within himself. The foregoing practices will have given him a great insight into his own nature (and, incidentally, into that of others) and he will find within himself things the existence of which he had never suspected previously. Much of what he sees will be of a highly unpleasant sort, for, if it is true that within us all is a God, it is no less true that there is a devil there as well, a devil that is latent in even the most saintly of ordinary men. But, however horrible a form it may wear and however aghast he may feel at the realization of its presence within him, whatever he sees in his heart must be faced with perfect sincerity and fearlessness. If we run away, shutting our eyes to the horror or denying its existence, all further progress is blocked. Our hearts will then become, not quiet temples in which we can live in peace and serenity, but haunted houses thronged by ghosts, the horrors that we know exist and yet refuse to face. Whatever is within us must be contemplated with a calm gaze; if it is harmful it must be overcome and destroyed, but never under any circumstances must it be feared or run away from with shocked denials of its presence, else we shall have to say with Job: 'That which I greatly feared has come upon me.' Moreover, this is as true of outer situations that give rise to fear as it is of inner tendencies that the mind cannot face. Both alike must be overcome.

The method for overcoming them is the one which has been outlined above. The intuition guided mind must be used as both compass and rudder to control the riotous phantasizing of the inner senses, and, that being controlled, the outer sense life will come under control as well, just as the whole body of a horse is directed merely by turning his head. To give just one example, many aspirants fight a continuous losing battle against their sex desires simply because they try to control the outward manifestations while allowing the inner phantasy to play freely. The more they check themselves without, the more riotously surges the phantasy within, whereas, if they would first control the latter, the former would come quite naturally and easily to heel.

Finally, the aspirant should take care to guard himself against any feeling of disappointment. This is one of the greatest snares on the path. The path is an arduous one, for the whole personality has to be remade so that it is centred above and not below. When we consider the countless lives we have spent upon the downward path and the fact that our whole environment, social, literary and scientific, is, in the majority of cases, of such a nature that it hinders rather than helps our struggles, it is small wonder that progress should be slow. All round us are those who say that the task is an impossible, even a chimerical one, and urge us to be content with life of the senses. Even the so-called religious people are of little help, for they say one thing with their lips but fear its opposite within their hearts. That is why it is inevitable that, from time to time, grey and despondent thoughts should steal into the heart, whispering that in all these years of practice no progress has been made.

But the seductive whispers are false, and he who has strengthened his mind by yoga knows that they are false. If he will follow his proper technique and examine the causes for the rising of these moods, he will find that they invariably arise from self-centred thoughts, hankerings after recognition, supernormal powers and other outward shows, which have taken advantage of a weakened mental control – perhaps through fatigue or slight ill-health – to revenge themselves for past suppression by blackening everything within their reach. Essentially the mechanism is the same as that seen in the small boy (and would it were only in small boys!) who becomes peevish and 'will not play' because, in reality, some cherished and unspoken desire of his has been thwarted. Here again, the strengthening of the mind by constant practice of the yogic technique is the great remedy for these black moods.

The finest timber comes from the slowest growing trees. He who expects to blossom into a yogi in a few months or even in a few years of practice is bound to be disappointed and had better leave the whole subject alone. He, however, who has the sincerity and courage to face whatever is in him, the persistence to go on with his struggle in the face of obstacles within and without, and the humility to recognize that all that he has done is to take the first few steps on a tremendous journey, is certain to achieve something which he would not give away in exchange even for the whole world, for, as Sri Krishna teaches in the Gitā, even the seeker after yoga goes far beyond the hopes and fears of ordinary religion and 'even a little of this *dharma* delivers from great fear'.

2. Symbolism and Knowledge

All over the world and in all ages there has been a tradition of a wonderful hidden Knowledge and of a secret Path that led to that Knowledge. In acient India young men in hundreds cut themselves adrift from home ties and from the claims of orthodox religion to wander in forests and among inaccessible mountains in search of it. In Greece and Egypt men sought it through initiation into the Mysteries, and, even during the ages when the Roman Catholic Church held well-nigh undisputed sway in Europe, there were men, and even organized bodies of men, who, under the guise of alchemical researches, pursued the same quest. And then there was the chivalric quest for the Holy Grail, a genuine fragment of the ancient, pre-Christian initiatory tradition, though the Church found it expedient superficially to Christianize the symbols and then to take it under its wing.

Even among what are called primitive tribes, to this day there are mystic Initiations and men who lay aside bow and spear and all that savage standards hold worth living for to pursue a quest which they are scarcely able to formulate. Sir James Fraser reports secret societies in Africa whose members are resurrected after a magic sleep. Their members are taught the rudiments of a secret language, and in one, at least, the initiates are known as *nganga*, the Knowing Ones.*

Anthropologists and psychologists think they know all about these initiations, and pretty small beer they make of them. All one can do is to say with Job: 'Doubtless ye are the people and wisdom shall surely die with ye, but we also have understanding.'

It is simply not true that Osiris is a vegetation, or Apollo a solar myth. Rather, if we must talk like this, we should say that vegetation

*See *The Golden Bough* (Baldur the Beautiful), Chapter 11.

is an Osiris myth and the sun a myth of Apollo, since Apollo and Osiris and all such names refer to facts of a higher order than those with which physical scientists deal. Just because of this it is impossible that physical science should ever lay hold on them; the meshes of its net are so coarse that nothing but physical facts can be caught in them. The superphysical facts to which these and other similar names refer have been symbolized in a variety of ways, chiefly by those great natural processes which are fitting symbols, just because they are physical plane manifestations of the same inner processes to which the symbols refer. But no mistake could be greater than to take the symbols – corn, phallus, sun, and what-not – *as we perceive them*, for the things symbolized.

It is not intended here to unveil the content of the Mysteries, even were it possible to do so to the uninitiated. The Knowledge exists, and those who seek it rightly and with perfect sincerity find out its existence for themselves. Science sets out to give a coherent account of such aspects of the universe as are presented (at this particular epoch) to our physical senses, and with such an account we can have no quarrel. But when scientists put forward an explicit or implicit claim that such knowledge is the only real knowledge, that the world of the physical senses is the only real world, we can only say that it is false and that their world is the outermost skin of reality. Nor can we agree to the physicist's idea that the world of sense, with all its colours, sounds, and tastes, is a mere appearance of a grey world of colourless, tasteless, soundless, featureless matter, and still less with the view that reality is a set of mathematical equations, a complex of formal structures. To the exponents of this last view we must ask: structures of what? Equations about what? There can be no equations devoid of content, and to think that there can be is to be guilty of what Whitehead terms 'the fallacy of vacuous actuality'. We must always remember that, as he says, 'apart from the experiences of subjects, there is nothing, nothing, bare nothingness'.*

We have spoken of a hidden Knowledge, and the question naturally arises as to where that Knowledge is to be found. Is it to be sought for in books or records, either known to us, or hidden in

*A. N. Whitehead, Process and Reality, Macmillan.

secret libraries away from the eyes of common men? It is certainly true that attempts have been made to express it in writing and in other media; in writings which are accessible to all men, as well as in writings that are not so accessible. Accessible or inaccessible, such books are not the Knowledge, cannot in themselves impart the Knowledge, and, in a sense, do not even contain it; they can only help to lead us to the Knowledge. It may even be said that until we have at least some portion of the Knowledge, we cannot understand the books.

Perhaps an illustration from the field of art will be of use. Beauty exists, and artists perceive it. Seeing it, they are compelled to try and express it. Nevertheless, no work of art can give final expression to it: always the artist must be continuing his efforts, never resting content with his results. Neither can he impart that beauty to others, except is so far as they themselves are, or are potentially, awake to its perception.

So it is with the Knowledge. Only he in whose heart its shoots are already sprouting can read the books which express it, for they are all written in a cipher, a cipher which is the more difficult to read because it has all the outward appearance of being written in our own language. A moment's thought will suffice to show that this must be so; all the books in the world fundamentally refer to data derived from physical sense experience, and if they are to express those far greater aspects of reality that are beyond the level of the senses, it can only be by symbolism that they can do so. This is as true of books that employ an abstract 'philosophical' symbolism as it is of those that luxuriate in a tropical forest of what everyone recognizes as symbols. Hence it follows that those modern thinkers who attempt to reach truth by tying words down to their meanings in and for (sense) experience by stripping them of the felt aura which surrounds their clear reference, and however useful such a procedure may be in certain limited fields, are going in the opposite direction to that which leads to the Knowledge.

This knowledge [says Plato] is not a matter that can be transmitted in writing, like other sciences. It requires long continued intercourse between pupil and teacher, in joint pursuit of the object they are seeking to apprehend; and then, suddenly, just as light flashes forth when a fire is kindled, this knowledge is born in the soul and henceforth nourishes itself . . . But I do not think a public 'inquiry', as it is called, into these ultimate matters would be of any benefit – except to a very few, and these are men who would be able, with a little explanation, to discover the truth for themselves.*

The Knowledge exists in the only place where knowledge can exist, namely, in that which is the knower. Within the unsounded deeps of man's being is all knowledge, for within him is hidden that Power which has brought all this universe into manifestation. For the same reason it is within all that exists, and not in man alone. The minutest centre of life, the amoeba if you like, or the smallest unit of so-called inorganic matter, is a manifestation of that same Power, and within it is the Knowledge in all its fullness. If it be true, as Eddington has said, that a single electron occupies the whole of space, it is only true because there is that in the electron which knows the whole of space with all its multitudinous contents.

Nevertheless, in saying this we must not think that the Knowledge is consciously present to these tiny atoms of life, nor even to the great majority of those bigger units that we call men. We know from our own experience that what is actually and overtly known to us in the sunshine of normal waking consciousness is very little indeed. We do not know (whatever astronomers may believe) the constitution of the stars; we do not know what happens to the psyche after the death of the body; we do not know even what is taking place in the next room. In our ordinary consciousness, in fact, we know so little that it is almost nothing, and yet is is only because all knowledge is within us that we are able to play our parts in the universe with all its stars and lives and rooms. Everything in the cosmos is linked to everything else in a wonderful network of relations; and that means that everything knows or, as Whitehead puts it, 'prehends' everything else. For, in the last analysis, there is no meaning in what philosophers term 'relations' except as acts of knowledge. If it is true (and it certainly is) that my body is related to that of the star known as Sirius, it is because, and only because,

*Plato's Seventh Epistle (Morrow's translation). Some critics have doubted the genuineness of these epistles, though others, equally scholarly, accept them. Someone wrote these words – it may have been Jack the Giant Killer for all I care – and they are the truth.

there is that in me which knows Sirius, and that in Sirius which knows me. All the stuff about electro-magnetic fields is, *apart from the knower of those fields*, sheer nonsense.

We are all familiar with philosophical writers who propound theories of a truly wonderful sort. Some of us were fascinated by those theories when we first heard them. When Berkeley told us that so-called material things were in reality ideas in the mind of God, when Hegel told us that the real was the rational and that the only true reality was the Absolute Idea, or when Bergson championed intuition as the source of real knowledge, we naïvely supposed that these eminent writers meant what they said and had something important to impart to us. We thought that if we mastered the difficulties of their thought, we should really learn something that we had not known before, should expand our consciousness and see the universe in ways quite different from those familiar to us. Disappointment was in store for us. We soon found that the philosophers were not talking of any experience that they had had or even that they hoped to have.

'This table,' said my philosophy professor one day to me, 'is really a colony of souls, bound together into a community by love.' It was wonderful! It was thrilling! But when we wanted to learn more about those souls, to learn how we could know and enter into communion with those of our fellow men, we were led off again into the labyrinth of words, and found that we were not to be vouchsafed any more intimate experience of the table than falls to the lot of any diner off it, nor, if power was our aim, were we to gain any power of manipulation over it that was not possessed by the merest carpenter or chemist.

The table in fact remained what it always had been, something to eat one's dinner on. And gradually some of us came to realize that that was all it was to the professor himself, and that in truth the whole soaring structure of his idealism was just an edifice of words, a verbal Tower of Babel. We read Bradley and learned that Time was riddled with contradictions and could not be said to have real existence. It was mere 'appearance', and behind it somewhere was Reality.

But where was the Reality, and how were we to establish ourselves in it? Did Bradley know anything real of it himself? It seemed that the question was thought a little vulgar. It was as if one had mentioned an aperient at the drawing-room tea table. It was all very disappointing: the thrilling words meant nothing at all. Plato had said somewhere that a thing's existence was its power to act. These systems of philosophy, did they have any power to act? Could they help one to gain control over the outer world of nature? Oh no! We were politely and a little scornfully referred to science. Could they help us to master the inner world of our souls? Oh dear no! That was the province of religion. What then could they do? Nothing at all, it seemed, except develop a skill in verbal dialectic, which, however fascinating to some minds, had little more significance than the equally fascinating skill of the chess player. It was all bogus: as bogus as the teachings of the churches which safely promised knowledge after death; in some ways even more bogus, since one gathered that most of the philosophers did not feel at all sure that there was any 'after-death', and certainly did not know anything about it.

No doubt many people will think all this inconceivably naïve; the real questions that man wishes to address to the Sphinx of nature always do seem childish to our academics. From one point of view we might describe the whole process of academic education as a learning to substitute the unreal and artificial questions of the abstracting for the real and vital questions of the integral psyche. At any rate, it will be clear to academic minds that we ought never to have indulged in these 'romantic' desires for a transcendental knowledge. In the Middle Ages such Faustian hankerings were thought to involve a wicked relationship with the Devil: nowadays the Freudians tell us that they are due to an equally wicked intimacy with our mothers! In any case, we are certain to be told that our search is a vain one, since no such knowledge exists or ever has existed. Its existence, in fact, is a childish phantasy, entirely comparable to that of the pot of gold to be found at the foot of the rainbow. (Incidentally, there *is* a pot of gold at the foot of the rainbow, but it is at the far end, and no mere academic has ever reached it.)

It is not so, however, and those who seek it resolutely enough find it now as in former ages. Porphyry relates in his Life of Plotinus how the latter at the age of twenty-eight sought for it in the lecture rooms of all the most famous philosophers of Alexandria, at that time the great philosophical centre of the Western world. Always he came away from them 'saddened and discouraged' by what he had heard until one day at the recommendation of a friend he went to Ammonius Saccas, the 'God-Taught'. After hearing only one lecture, he recognized that he had found his teacher. The Fire of which Plato writes in his epistle, quoted earlier, flashed in his soul, and, exclaiming 'this is the man for whom I was looking', he attached himself to Ammonius and remained his pupil for eleven years.

What exactly it was that Ammonius taught is not known to us, as he left no writings and his pupils were bound to secrecy. But the teacher can be known by the pupil, and if we study Plotinus, we can be certain that what his master taught was no mere intellectual chess-play of the sort that had driven him away from the other teachers, but was one of the many recensions of the deathless Knowledge which he sought. 'Out of discussion we call to vision; to those desiring to see we point the path; our teaching is a guiding in the way; the seeing must be the very act of him who has made the choice.'* This is the authentic voice of the Inner Teaching. About eight hundred years previously the Buddha had said exactly the same: 'By yourself must the effort be made; the Buddhas are only Teachers. They who have entered on and tread the inner Path are liberated from the enslaving bonds of Death.'†

This inner Path is literally the path of *dhyāna* or 'meditation', but a broader rendering of the term is preferable, as the word meditation means different things to different people. To some it means a devotional musing on some 'holy' topic, to others a ruminative process of thought, and to still others a forcible concentration of mind upon one mental object. In the broadest sense, however, it refers to the Sacred Voyage up the river of our being to the Snowy Mountains from which that River takes its rise.

There are various means by which that Voyage can be made. Some of them suit one temperament and some suit another, but in

*Plotinus, 6.9.4.
†*Dhammapada*, 276.

all cases the actual Voyage is the same. We must leave behind the populous cities with their busy life, pass through the jungle tracts infested with dangerous animals, somehow or other cross the great mountain range, and reach the sacred Mānas Lake, the source of all the rivers. Thence if we seek the real Source, we must grow wings and follow the Swan's Path through the upper air.

This Voyage up the River of Life is no mere poetry, but a real voyage. It is the truth which underlies the ancient travels of Herakles, Odysseus, and Arjuna, and which inspires from within the arduous pilgrimages still made by millions in the East. It is even the archetype which shines before the inner eye of explorers, an archetype which, through projection into the physical world, invests with something of its own self-luminosity the sandy caravan routes across deserts and the snowy passes of the mountains so that they shine with a magic glamour which analytic realism tries in vain to assure us has no actual existence.

But it is not across physical deserts and mountains that the real Journey has to be made. As the Buddha has said:

Where, friend, one is neither born, grows old, or dies, neither leaves one sphere of existence, nor is reborn in another, that End of the World, I say, thou art not able to know, to see, or to arrive at by any walking. But neither do I say, friend, that without having reached that End of the World there can be any cessation of sorrow. Truly I tell you that within this fathom long body with its perceptions and its mind lies the world, its arising and its ceasing and the Way that leads to its cessation.*

And we can compare this with the words of Plotinus:

This is not a journey for the feet; the feet can only bring us from land to land; nor need you think of coach or ship to carry you away; all this order of things you must set aside and refuse to see. You must close the eyes and call instead upon another vision which is to be waked within you, a vision, the birthright of all, but which few turn to use. †

Nevertheless, the Way is a real way, and one on which there are landmarks which may be recognized by all who tread it, now as

*Samyutta Nikāya, 1.59.
†Plotinus, 6.8.

formerly. The Upanishadic seer, Yajñavalkya, relates the following verses which were ancient even in his time:

The ancient, subtle, and far-leading Path has been touched and found by me. By it the wise Knowers of the Brahman, liberated from the bonds of earth, travel upwards to the heavenly world. On it, they say, are white and blue, yellow and green and red. This was the Path found by Brahmā himself.*

We should note here how Yajñavalkya refers to it as a teaching that had come to him in the form of an ancient, traditional verse, and how the unknown writer of the verse refers to it as being still more ancient than himself. And yet, to this day the landmarks remain the same, so that anyone who treads it can recognize the meaning of the cryptic statement about the colours.

Many who study mystical literature from outside think that because the descriptions of the Path vary, they therefore refer to different paths, and some even make the further inference that they are 'purely subjective'. But no conclusion could be further from the truth. The teachings of all genuine seers are in reality in complete agreement; it is only the verbal descriptions which vary. All descriptions, whether those of ordinary common-sense or those of so-called exact science, are symbolic. The words refer to something beyond themselves, something whose nature they can only suggest.

There is a story of a small boy who was being given a lesson in elementary astronomy by his teacher. Having been told that such and such a star was Sirius, and such another Aldebaran, the boy became thoughtful and asked, 'How do we know that those are their names?' It is doubtless a truism, but it is one which we too often forget in practice, namely, that words mean only what we have agreed that they shall mean.†

The work of scientists is seen to refer to a common body of experience because we have hammered out a common terminology. If, instead of being in very general touch with one another, scien-

---

Brihadāranyaka Upanishad, 4.4.8.
†The above is said without reference to the theory of Mantra and of True Name, discussion of which here would be irrelevant and would lead us too far afield.

tists had to work in little, independent groups, scattered in time and space, each group evolving its own terminology, it would by no means be easy to correlate their researches, though it would always be possible for one who had both sufficient first-hand experience of science and sufficient patience.

The writings of seers are in a somewhat similar case to such hypothetical scientific studies. They are the products of isolated individuals or groups of individuals, often quite out of touch with similar groups elsewhere, and each of them has used such terms to describe his experience as were suggested by the tradition with which he was most familiar. The result often appears chaotic; but anyone who cares to follow the Path for himself will soon find that the chaos is only apparent, and that the various terms used in any one system are easily translatable into those of another. There will not always be a one to one correspondence, for the groupings of experiences under one head is also largely a personal matter. Whether a given complex of experience is to be taken as a whole or divided into aspects which are given various names is a matter which will vary with the point of view of each individual experiencer.

In the ancient world such ability to translate from one symbolism into another seems to have been more common than it is at present. We read how Greek priests could visit Egypt or Chaldaea and at once recognize a given 'foreign' God as a correspondence of such and such a Greek one. The equation of Thoth with Hermes is a well-known example, but it is by no means unique. It was possible for any initiated priest of the ancient religions to wander, like Apollonius, over the whole world and recognize his own Gods wherever he went.

The decay of this ability seems to have been connected with the development, somewhere in the first millennium B.C., of the power of abstract thought. Such thought is itself a symbolism, as philosophers are now once more beginning to realize. It is a symbolism, and a very powerful one for certain purposes, but it seems to carry with it a fatal tendency to take itself too seriously and to pose as being more than symbolism. To say that the world is a product of the union of consciousness with content-form is no less symbolic and no more true than to say that it is the marriage of the sun and moon, the union of the Sky God with the Earth Mother; and to say that the universe is an interrelatedness of atoms is as definitely symbolic a statement as that it is the morning stars singing together.

The trouble arises when, because of their great usefulness in certain fields, we take the former type of statement as something more than it is. We tend to take the description in abstract terms as being actual truth, while we relegate the field of concrete symbolism to poetry; and the art of taking poetry seriously is one which, despite all the poetry which has been written, the West has definitely and almost completely lost. The result of this devaluation of one set of symbols is to render ourselves largely incapable of reading them or of thinking accurately with their help. This is a great misfortune because, while it is true that the abstract symbols employed by modern science and philosophy have great flexibility and precision (though less of this latter quality than we are apt to think) the concrete ones are infinitely richer in feeling-content, and feeling-content alone is what can save us from the grey and featureless ghosts of billiard-ball atoms.

The ability to read and think in terms of concrete symbols is of very great importance, for it prevents that vicious abstraction of all value from experience which is so marked a feature of the purely scientific world view. We may compare the two to trade by barter and trade by currency. The former is cumbersome and not very exact, but it is always in touch with realities and is not liable to be upset, as is currency, by sudden political revolutions or artificial manipulations. The symbolism of five thousand years ago is as valid today as when it was first written, while the abstract symbols of the last century have become almost valueless. Can anyone now read Kelvin or Spencer? The symbols of the archaic world are graven more indelibly than on any granite hillside; they still fill and activate the hearts of men; those of last century science merely cumber the less accessible shelves of our libraries.

From time to time it is necessary to translate the golden concrete symbols of the ancient writers into the abstract paper currency of modern thought. This, however, is because men no longer wear about their necks substantial gold chains from which they can bite off a link or two to settle their innkeeper's account; they are at home

c

only in the convenient but unstable world of cheque-books. But we must always remember that such translations from the language of eternity into the language of a day are essentially ephemeral. The butterflies of contemporary thought come and go in fluttering succession: the archaic eagles soar in the empyrean through unending cycles. Not Christ alone but every seer can say with truth: 'Heaven and earth shall pass away, but my words shall not pass away.'

In particular, the ability to read the concrete symbols is of the utmost importance to one striving to tread the Inner Path, a Path on which feeling and thought have to be fused into a unity. Any one-sidedness in this respect results in a tension in the psyche which will prevent harmonious growth and give rise either to a sterile intellectuality, masquerading as purely philosophic mysticism, or else to a somewhat infantile emotionalism, calling itself devotional religion. In both cases mystical experience may be gained, but it will be experience of an unbalanced sort which will bear in its very texture the stamp of its inadequacy.

One of the most unsatisfactory aspects of scholarly approaches to the subject is this modern inability to read concrete symbols and the consequent over-emphasis on words. In his work on Shankara and Eckhart, Otto discusses the question whether the Vedāntik Brahman, the Buddhist Nirvāna, and Eckhart's Godhead are the same or different. But what is different? The words, of course, are different: the groups of ideas referred to by the words are also different, to some extent at least. But that is not the end of the matter. That to which these words refer is neither a word nor an idea, and no one who thinks that it is can possibly come at the root of the matter. There are not half a dozen of these mystical absolutes floating about in the universe. There is not even one true and several false ones. There is just one Reality which has been symbolized in various ways, each symbol expressing more or less inadequately some one particular aspect of it. 'The Real is one; men describe it in many ways' (Rig Veda).

The writings of the seers cannot and must not be read as if they were so many sets of interesting ideas to be judged by their logical coherency. They are descriptions of experience; and the first necessity, if we would understand them, is to realize that their statements refer to something which is neither a word nor an 'idea'. The words of the seer are finger-posts pointing to experience, and we shall never understand them aright if we persist in interpreting them according to the method of academic philosophy, which is merely a logicalization and a drawing of inferences from the experience available to all in normal waking consciousness.

The range of the mystic extends far beyond the frontiers of this normal waking world, and only a seer can understand fully the words of another seer. Nevertheless, there is a means by which a partial understanding can be gained, and that is through the intuition, a faculty which is an object of dispute to the learned, an object of cultivation to the wise. Space forbids our entering on any discussion of this faculty, the certainty-giving *buddhi* of Indian teachings; we will only say that it is a power which depends upon the unity of the whole cosmos, upon the fact that any portion of the universe, even the smallest, reflects in its structure the pattern of the whole. The structure of experience-levels far beyond our normal range is mirrored in that of this level, and the process of intuition is essentially a reading of what is remote by the contemplation of what is near. This is the meaning of what is known as the Hermetic axiom, 'As above, so below', a universal teaching on the Inner Path, a key which will open any lock within the Cosmos. This axiom is to be found in the teachings of all the mystical schools. Three instances may be given.

Neo-Platonic:	'All that is yonder is also Here'. (Plotinus)
Kabbalistic:	'Esoterically the man below corresponds entirely to the Man Above'. (The *Zohar*)
Upanishadic:	'Whatever is here, that (also) is There. Whatever is There, that again is here'.

(Kathopanishad)

3. The Sacred Marriage

The essentially creative act is the union of opposites. In mere mathematics, the conjunction of a plus with an equal minus results in zero, but in the realm of real experience this is not so. The union of a positive with a negative results in the raying out of a new creation; in fact, it is in this way that all true creation takes place. As Blake puts it: 'Without contraries, there is no progression.' Out of the marriage of the light and dark halves of the soul, the wonderful new birth, the spiritual birth, takes place, a thing which cannot happen so long as we artificially isolate one half of ourselves, calling it good, respectable, etc. Such isolation of all that we approve in ourselves, to the exclusion of all the rest, leads and can only lead to psychic sterility.

We are afraid of all that is dark within ourselves, not realizing that it is but the shadow of what is light and therefore inseparable from it. The wisdom that is hidden in ancient myths should have sufficed to warn us of the misfortune that pursues the man who has 'lost his shadow'. It will be objected that the Gods cast no shadows. That is quite true, but Gods are not men. In their case the shadows which are their counterparts have their separate or semi-separate existence, and that is one reason for the teaching that Gods must become men, uniting light with shadow, before they can achieve the goal of liberation. In man, the universal divine powers came to a focus, and therefore in his heart there must always be darkness as well as light.

But we are afraid of the dark as such; we people it with bogies, which then terrify us more. Because of our fear of what is dark in our hearts, the dark itself becomes hostile to us, though its hostility is in truth but the projection of our own fears. It becomes to us the dark unknown, the dwelling of the terrible dragon-woman, the eater-up of children, the witch, sinister and evil. We seek to flee away, but forever she follows us as our shadow, and instead of our psychic energy's being poured forth in creation, it is drained away in wastage behind.

Yet, if we but turn round and face the shadow, everything is changed. The devouring nightmare becomes the source of inspiration, the malignant witch becomes the beneficent goddess, and from the union of light and darkness shines a radiance that is beyond all that we know as light, 'a Light that never was on Sea or Land'.

How does this work out in practice? That which we love draws us ever upwards, outwards into the light; but that which we hate, the shadow of what we love, draws us equally backward with its bond of fear. That which we seek lures us onwards; at the same time, all that is not included in that 'sought' seeks us in turn and pulls us back towards it. We seek the sun, but we ourselves are sought by the moon; and between these two forces we are held in motionless sterility.

The sun is the light of life, but the moon is the light of wisdom which shines at its full when in opposition to the sun. Hence it is that, in order to find wisdom, we must follow the example of Nachiketas, the hero of the *Kathopanishad*, and plunge boldly into the death kingdoms of the night; for it is only there that we can learn of the secret causes which govern the phenomena of life, the hidden currents which carry forward the ship of the psyche. It was on the full-moon night that the Buddha gained full enlightenment and saw deep into the causes of things; it was also on a full moon night, that of Vaishakha, that he was born and also left his home to seek the Truth.

These two full moons have different meanings, for, in the interval between the two, the polarity of the heavens has been entirely reversed. In the language of astrology we may say that at the first, the Vaishakha moon of birth and going forth, the sun was in Aries, the sign of life, and the moon in Libra or the Balance; while at the time of the Enlightenment, the *Sharat Purnimā* (according to certain traditions), it was the other way round, the sun in Libra, being balanced between day and night, and the moon in Aries in the house of life.

Thus are exemplified the Bhagavad-Gita's words about what

is day to the many being night to the seer, and vice versa. The union of opposites is the great principle of the inner life. It is useless to imagine that we can have the one pole without the other, for all that happens is that in our frenzied efforts to isolate and develop the one, we bring about an automatic degradation of the other, which thereby becomes ugly and our enemy.

Let us consider this in the concrete. The state we know as greed is one of the distinctly unpleasant aspects of human nature. But what is greed, and how does it arise? There are two processes in the psyche, just as there are two in the universe; one a giving out and the other a taking in. For good reasons these two have been symbolized since ancient times by the outgoing and ingoing breath; and the moment we have said this we are forced to realize that the two are entirely interdependent. Both of them are necessary and should be, as in yogic breathing, entirely balanced. The one is as necessary to psychic and physical health as the other.

Greed, then, is a manifestation, a distorted manifestation, of the in-breath. If that manifestation has become something ugly and sorrow-producing, it can only be because the corresponding out-breath has been emphasized in some exaggerated and one-sided way. We must not be misled by the commonplace antithesis of giving and getting, in which one is considered 'good' and the other 'bad'. If our getting has become ugly, it is because our giving has become unwise and unbalanced.

The process of giving, the out-breath, is the projection of ourselves upon the universe around us. To breathe upon a person or animal is one of the ancient magical ways of establishing our power over him, of bringing him under our control. This alone is sufficient to show us where we have gone wrong. We give (in the most general sense) in order that we may thereby bind the recipients of our gifts to ourselves; in other words, that we may bring them under our control. It is for this reason that so much so-called charity and philanthropy is offensive, and that Patanjali warns would-be yogis against the receiving of gifts.

Looked at in this way, the process of giving, as it is usually practised, is just as ugly as that of getting; but we are so hypnotized by the conventional over-valuation of giving that we indiscriminatingly label it 'good' and fail to see that it can be as definitely egoistic as its opposite, getting. And yet we all recognize the unsatisfactory nature of the 'millionaire's charity', and perceive the hidden selfishness of the man who, with a tense fanaticism, insists on 'doing good' to his fellows.

There is no use, then, in trying to root our greed from our natures by making a direct attack on it. Greed is merely an exaggeration of one of the essential movements of our nature, a movement that in itself is perfectly healthy and absolutely necessary to manifested life on any plane. If we wish to destroy its ugliness and harmfulness, we must first find out what is the exaggeration which has brought about the morbid condition, and to do that, as we have seen, means looking in the opposite quarter of the heavens, the opposite pole of the psyche. Instead of the forceful, ego-directed out-breathing which is designed to influence and control others, we should breathe out calmly and in detachment, just because it is our nature to breathe out. Giving should be a process which streams out from us as easily and naturally as light streams out from the sun, unattached to the objects it falls upon, and indifferent to whether it is received by the earth or is 'lost in space'. To the extent to which we can achieve such giving, we shall find that our greed (as we know it) has vanished, leaving in its place something which no one would think of calling greed, but which is, nevertheless, its healthy and real substratum, the process of breathing in or getting.

In Sanskrit these two processes are known as *Yoga-Kshema,* a compound which has been used in various senses, but of which the first part, *yoga,* signifies the out-going breath which unites with (*yuj*) or projects into things, and *kshema,* the getting or safe preservation of what is acquired. The yogi, as the Bhagavad-Gita tells us, is to be *niryoga-kshema,* beyond or detached from these two. This detachment he gains by the characteristic yogic technique of harmonizing the out-breath with the in-breath, a process which it is utterly stupid to take on the physical level alone.

Let us take another pair of opposites, the most fundamental of all, the pair known as life and death. Why is it that death is so ugly and gloomy to us? To term a person or thing 'deathly' is to say the worst thing that can be said of him or it. A thing may be deadly causing death to others, and still appear beautiful, but if we give it the adjective 'deathly', we have given it the ugliest term we know. And yet death is but the shadow of life, and can therefore only derive its ugliness from an ugliness in the life which throws the shadow, or, rather, in our attitude to and conception of that life. Once more, life is the out-breath, death its corresponding intake. Life is the sun, positive, active, and male; death is the moon, negative, receptive, and female. It is true that in another sense life is assimilation or intake, and death an outgoing, a 'passing on', but this contradiction is only apparent and in reality supports our general statement, for it shows the presence in each of its opposite. It is a well-known saying that death is eternal life, and we may add with no less truth that eating is dying.* With every mouthful of food that we eat, and not only gross physical food, we are taking death into ourselves. Hence the statement that the yogi who seeks to conquer death should abstain from all food. The actual states that we know as life and death are compound states, resultants of the interaction of the two poles. Death gnaws at the heart of life, while life triumphs in the very midst of death.

> Blow bugles, blow, set the wild echoes flying!
> And echo answers, dying, dying, dying.

Death is the Isis upon whose unveiled face no man has ever looked, for her throne is beyond the boundaries of manifested being, as, indeed, is the throne of life. No man has ever truly gazed upon life or death as they are in themselves, but only upon the various interactions of the two which constitute the whole of the manifested universe.

It is the failure to recognize this inevitable intertwining of life and death that is the cause of death's appearing so terrible to us. We avidly pursue life, and therefore we are ourselves pursued by the sinister figure of death. We long for life, stretch out our arms to it, project ourselves into it, and therefore death longs for us,

*In both Hindu and Buddhist tradition there are four types of *āhāra* or food. These are usually misunderstood to mean four types of physical food, whereas, in truth, one is physical or material and the other three are what is termed 'superphysical'.

reaches forth *his* arms to grasp us, lies in wait for us at every turn, and draws us to himself. We are living, we are life, we are the sun, we triumph, we radiate around, asserting ourselves in the face of the Cosmos. We banish from ourselves all that militates against life. A million men are dying and countless millions have already died. Away with such pale ghosts! Let them be gone from our sight! Triumphantly we use our intellects, those willing tools of our desires, to prove that there are and can be no such things as ghosts. We turn night into day, using all our scientific knowledge to light up the night, so that we never have to face the darkness nor even see the unresting turning of the wheel of fate above us in the heavens. And so, too, with that other night, the night of winter. Can we not cheat it by taking ship to the antipodes in search of summer? Can we not, even with the help of steel and steam and glass, make little private summers in our houses?

Assuredly, we are the masters of Fate! Men that love lightly may die, but we . . .? There shall be no night, no winter, and no death for us. A savage tribe kills a missionary in Africa; the tribe must be annexed and brought into our system. The river Thames floods its banks and drowns six people in London; this is an outrage, and the whole land clamours that the wanton river must be bitted. Disease carries away great numbers of us; at once we produce our treasured coins, those golden tokens of the golden solar disc, and pour them out in hospitals and in research, confident that with our overflowing life we shall succeed in banishing the hateful spectres. 'This foe has been slain by me, others also shall I slay tomorrow. I am the Ruler, the enjoyer; I am the accomplished one, powerful and happy. Thus, deluded by unwisdom.'

Deluded by unwisdom? Yes, assuredly. Do what we will, our fate, furious and hostile as a woman scorned, pursues us with implacable steps. And we –

Like one, that on a lonesome road doth walk in fear and dread,
And having once looked back, walks on and turns no more his head;
Because he knows a frightful fiend doth close behind him tread.

We press on, denying family, denying history, denying the whole magical eternity of the past in our frenzied efforts to escape. The fatal lunar arrows of cancer strike our bodies down in increasing numbers, and the same malignant witch shreds our minds into the tatters of neurosis and actual lunacy. Fear descends upon us, like a cold, poisonous fog, obscuring the beloved sun from our sight, so that we can no longer see our way in the darkness that wraps us round. Under our very feet the solid earth of our beautiful civilization opens in cracks and fissures from which, in answer to the lunar pull, come welling up the deep, abysmal waters which swirl around us, bringing madness with their touch.

It is no use. We cannot cheat the unity of Being. In-breath must follow out-breath; night must follow day; winter must follow summer; and death must follow life. We *must* turn round and face the moon with friendly, and not with timid eyes. We *must* cease from overvaluing and projecting all our phantasies upon life, if we are to escape being shattered by the echoes from the undervalued death. Let us remember that we have a back as well as a front, and that however bravely we may march forward, protected by the golden breastplate of the sun, our backs are none the less defenceless before the keen arrows of the moon who, as Artemis, hunts with her dogs in the dark forests of the night. It is for this reason that the stab in the back, treachery from our followers, the snake in the grass, and even the commonplace window at our back, or the reflection of someone behind us glimpsed in a mirror, are all, in varying degrees, objects of dread to us. Were not all the solar heroes thus smitten from behind? Remember Hercules dying of the treacherously given poisoned shirt, Siegfried stabbed in the back, Karna slain while his chariot wheels stuck fast in the mud, Akhenaten struck down by a lunar disease, Ra overcome by the poisonous snake set in his path by the guileful Isis, Agamemnon, king of men, slain in his triumph by his crafty wife, and Arthur perishing in mystic, sea-girt Lyonesse through the treachery of his own kinsman Mordred.

Deep in the caves of the soul is hidden the wisdom which alone can teach us to avoid this fate. There, in those caves, as in the ancient mysteries of Eleusis, must be brought about the sacred marriage of the sun and moon. Sri Ramchandra of the solar race must bow at the feet of Lunar Durga, if the *Vijaya* or victory is to be achieved.

And it is notable that the timeless wisdom of the Indian tradition begins the feast of the Great Goddess just one month before the moon of enlightenment that is to follow, the moon at which the 'Gates of Immortality' are opened wide for all who have the eye to see and the heart to follow.* At the festival of Dūrga, the sun is in the sign of marriage (Libra) and, as he sets upon the western horizon, the moon shines above him in the mid-heaven to receive his worship. Then, as the moon descends into opposition,† the sacred marriage is achieved, the tension from both becomes equal and opposite, and the soul, brought by those tensions to the very centre of the sphere of being, stands between day and night in poised serenity, master of Fate, lord of the mystic year.

That is what happens to him who can see the true moon, the moon of which our satellite is but a symbol, and, having seen, can face with fearless eyes her calm, immortal gaze and receive without shrinking the cold waters of the wisdom-dew which she sheds in his warm heart. Gently and imperceptibly that dew falls, cooling the fever of desire, each shining drop reflecting in its heart the cyclic, starry wheel of life and death that turns in calm, eternal majesty above it in the heavens.

Thus in the soul takes place the immaculate conception of the wisdom; immaculate, since neither man nor book have fathered it, but the eternal, all-embracing heaven, that heaven whose changeless, ever-changing rhythm is now imprinted on the petals of the soul. Till the end of time that imprint will endure, and against it neither life nor death will ever prevail. Never again will the soul breathe itself forth one-sidedly upon the waves of space, saying, in fiery, self-driven exultation, 'This universe am I; all this is mine.' But never, also, will it feel the grim reaction, the dark withdrawal of the ebbing sea, nor hear

*Approximately September–October. The date varies because of the lunar calendar. At Eleusis, the sacred marriage of the Great Mother was celebrated at approximately the same season.

†When in opposition to the sun, the moon is at the full. In astrological symbolism, the house of the marriage partner, the seventh, is opposite to the house of the native, the first, thus reflecting both the agreement of marriage and the conflict.

Its melancholy, long withdrawing roar,
Retreating to the breath
Of the night wind, down the vast edges drear
And naked shingles of the world.

Not that these two movements will cease in stone-like immobility. 'It is only for a brief moment that nature can be still.' As long as the universe shall last, so long will sun and moon weave out their mystic pattern of gold and silver on the loom of time, the pattern of in-breath and out-breath, the pattern of life and death. What changes is that no longer does the soul identify itself exclusively with the golden thread, and therefore is no longer forcibly seized by the other, the silver one; and no longer is that shining silver tarnished and blackened, as formerly, by the sulphur of desire. Instead, the starry wisdom of the night will blend with the living radiance of the day, so that the two form one harmonious pattern. As we read in the *Ishopanishad*: 'Projection and Withdrawal; he who knows these two together, by knowledge of Withdrawal having passed beyond death, by knowledge of Projection gains immortality.'* Or, in the symbolism we have adopted here, to one who knows the moon, death is no longer what it is to most, a thing of fear and terror, while, by the knowledge of the living sun, the soul enjoys eternity of life.

Thus is wisdom conceived in the depths of the soul by the union of opposites, the sacred marriage of the sun and moon. Before its actual birth or manifestation there is still some time that must elapse. Did not the Buddha himself, after his enlightenment, spend several weeks sitting under the mystic trees in profound peace before commencing his actual teaching?

This, too, is indelibly inscribed in the bright symbols of the heavens above us. A fortnight after the full moon of Wisdom, comes the dark, moonless night of *Diwāli*, the festival of Lights, which corresponds to All Hallow's E'en. The moon has joined the sun in the sign of the Balance, and in that darkness strange things take place. It is the night of magic, the night when all the souls of the dead come thronging to the world of men to visit and unite in

---

**Sambhūti and *Vināsha*: often translated as creation and destruction.

friendship with those who now dwell there. These souls or ghosts, who are the spirits of the womb of time, the past that has been lived and yet still lives, come to the embodied soul with a message of its solidarity with all that has gone before. It is by standing on the shoulders of a thousand vanished ages, profiting by the sacrifices of a million vanished lives, that the soul has reached its present poise of wisdom. Must it not then have a duty to perform, the duty of handing on its wisdom to the lives that are yet to come, so that thereby the past may be linked with the future by the living bonds of experience? Deep in the soul itself are all those vanished lives, and there, too, are those as yet unborn. The continuity must not be broken, and therefore, out of the magical darkness, the voice of a suffering past, the voice of all who have lived, suffered, and died, in order that the soul may stand where it now does, rises from the depths with its message of duty. 'Out of the silence that is peace a resonant voice shall arise. And this voice will say: It is not well; thou hast reaped, now thou must sow. And knowing this voice to be the silence itself, thou wilt obey' (*Light on the Path*).

This is the mysterious quickening of the inner birth, and shortly after, just as the sun is about to enter Scorpio, the sign of death and of mystic rebirth, there comes the festival of the divine birth, the birth of *Kārtikeya* the Beautiful,* the glorious son of fire and water, who, fostered by the wives of the Seven Rishis (the seven stars of the Great Bear or Plough) became commander of the heavenly host. Mounted on the peacock of the starry heavens, his twelve hands showing his mastery of the twelve-bodied wheel of fate, armed with the bow of yogic will, he slays the demon *Tāraka*, enemy of the Gods. Just so in ancient Egypt did the youthful, falcon-headed Horus, divine son of the dead Osiris, slay Set, the malignant demon of the dark.

*The *Krittika*, from which the name *Kārtikeya* derives, are the Pleiades, corresponding to one of the twenty-seven lunar asterisms or mansions that mark the moon's course along the ecliptic. Once considered the first, marking the beginning of the lunar year, this asterism is personified as *Kārtikeya*, Lord of the heavenly hosts of stars. Like many other archaic festivals, the festival of *Kārtikeya* dwindled with the rise of the great theistic cults which rose to popularity for their greater human appeal, sometimes at a sacrifice of the occult significance which invested all the older symbolisms.

Thus is brought about the sacred birth in which, as we learn from the ancient Mystery tradition, the Initiator dies in handing on the Word to his spiritual son. And thus we return to our starting point, the new and magical creation that results from the union of opposites. In following it up, we have wandered round heaven and earth, and perhaps have dazzled our eyes in the contemplation of great, starry beings whose cycles are the light of all the worlds. Nevertheless, the principle involved is of the utmost practical importance to ourselves, even in ordinary life. Our lives, no less than those of such great beings, are woven of the tissue of the opposites, and it is for us to learn that not by the attempted suppression of one of them in favour of the other, but by the balance and harmonious interplay of both, can we, ceasing to be mere 'processions of Fate', live creatively, and, breaking away from the weary and sorrow laden wheel, advance some steps towards the goal of freedom.

There will be those who, if they have had the patience to read so far, will ask impatiently what it is all about. What are those suns and moons, these births and marriages? What do they all mean? Cannot the matter, if any matter exist behind this swirl of words, be set forth plainly and simply? To such it can only be replied that these are the symbols carved upon the doorway of the temple, however imperfect may be the transcription here. He who would pass within (and there is no compulsion) must gain the power to read them for himself, for, if without that power he set foot within the gates, he will inevitably be lost in a whirl of illusions. Secondly, it must be stated that the so-called plain language of modern thought is a language of the mind alone, while the knowledge that is sought is the knowledge that belongs to the soul. Hence the uselessness in these realms of the spurious clarity of a language merely rooted in the mind, and the necessity for learning to read and use the language of concrete symbol which is, as it has always been, the language of the deeper psychic levels.

4. The Forgotten Land

The problem of what happens after death has at all times vexed the hearts of men. Many consider it insoluble to us on earth, a problem whose answer, if any, we shall know only when we have passed through the dark gateway and entered the 'undiscovered country from whose bourne no traveller returns'. This, however, is an illusion, comparable to the feeling that on the other side of that last ridge of blue hills lies the Happy Land, or, at least, a land where life is different and more beautiful than it is on this side. Alas, the valleys beyond the mountains differ only in commonplace ways from the familiar ones. He who has not understood the enigmatic, two-faced Sphinx of being here on this earth must not expect the answer to 'the great question' merely by virtue of having died. There, as here, he will behold but one of the two faces that we know as life and death. Only he who can see both at once, reading the riddle, is enthroned upon the Sphinx.

The various religions do not help us much in this enquiry. Yet they offer to give us definite information as to what happens after death, and it may, indeed, be worth our while to scan what they have to say, since much truth lies beneath their unfortunately discrepant accounts. The very discrepancies should put us on guard against taking any of their accounts too literally, and should force us to penetrate beneath the surface. This is the more necessary because the ignorance and cunning of priesthoods, the need for edification, and, it may be added, terrorization of the laymen, have mixed that truth with so much falsehood that only he who has an independent key can hope to find his way through the labyrinth.

Thus, Hindus and Buddhists have filled their sacred books with fairy-tales of men reborn as frogs and lizards,* while Christians

*The word fairy-tales is used deliberately, since those stories, false if taken literally, have, like fairy-tales, deep symbolic meanings.

appear to hold two incompatible beliefs at once. One Christian belief is that immediately after death they either ascend to the joys of heaven, or descend to be burnt for ever in hell; the other belief, held at the same time, is that they will sleep quietly in their graves until an event in the distant future, known as the Day of Judgement, after which the matter of heaven or hell will be decided.

Although 'our holy religion', whichever it may be, teaches us exactly what is going to happen to us, our quite unholy hearts secretly believe none of it; they may give an outer assent, but that is inevitably compensated by an inner denial.

Let us then leave the churches and turn to the spiritualists, those who, with the aid of mediums, profess to put us in touch with the spirits of the dead themselves. Here we find ourselves in a different atmosphere. The ancient scriptures, carved with the records of vanished seers, are gone, and we are shown into a darkened room in which a medium, sometimes of dubious antecedents, goes into more or less of a trance and, usually by automatic speech or writing, imparts messages and information which purport to come from one's deceased uncle, or, alternatively, from Oliver Cromwell or Julius Caesar. It is all very clear and definite – at least, it can be, if the medium be a good one – and, if we have lost the sombre dignity of the temple, we seem to have gained something of the vivid matter-of-factness of the laboratory or, at least, of the popular science magazine.

But, and this is the unfortunate aspect of the business, do these teachings really come from the discarnate spirits on whom they are fathered? What evidence have we in support of the claim? This question has been learnedly argued in many books, but, in the end, all we can say is that we do not know, and it seems that no one else really knows either. What is certain is that accounts given through different mediums are at least as discrepant with each other as are the teachings of the different religions, that they often bear the stamp of the medium's own unconscious mind, and that none of the ingenious tests devised by psychic researchers seem able to close the loopholes through which doubt may creep. Moreover, there is a curious psychic unhealthiness that pervades the séance room, an atmosphere to which, no doubt, one can get accustomed and cease to notice, as one can get used to the smell of bad drains – at one's own risk.

It is not intended to suggest that all mediums are given to trickery. Among their number are men and women of high idealism and great sincerity. Moreover, when all that is fraudulent has been set aside, psychical research has brought to light many genuine phenomena that are extremely interesting and quite unknown to orthodox science. So interesting and revolutionary are these facts that most orthodox scientists will go to any length rather than admit their existence. Nevertheless, the essential spiritist hypothesis, namely, that these super-natural manifestations are the work of spirits of the dead, remain, in the opinion of careful judges, unproved.

The physical sciences deal solely with physical bodies, and can therefore tell us in technical language only what we already know; namely, that our bodies are eaten by worms or burnt in fire and vanish utterly. As for academic philosophy, if anyone can find anything definite in its thick volumes of learned ifs and buts, he will be more fortunate than the present writer has been. There only remains psychology, but this science is still tethered by the heel to physiological concepts, nerves, brain structures, and the like. It is only just beginning to approach the psyche and psychic causation as independent realities.

Is there then no direction in which we may turn for information, is there no science which will help us? There is, but it is a science of which there are few serious students and still fewer masters. It is the most ancient of all the sciences, known by many names, from which we may select those of yoga, occultism, and magic, as being the best known. Despite all the books about it, it remains forever secret, since it is the science of the soul. Its instruments and experiments, no less than its data and conclusions are all within the soul and must be sought there in silence by each man for himself.

If, then, we attempt to render a few of its conclusions in terms of our shadowy intellectual concepts, it is not with the idea that such translations can constitute knowledge, but rather with the hope that even such poor and inadequate sketches may lure some reader into undertaking the voyage of exploration for himself.

Let us state at the outset that the soul has not once, but many times put on these garments of mortality, these coats of skin that we know as our bodies; it therefore does not have to speculate as to what may happen after the body's death; it knows it by experience. The soul, we repeat, *knows* what lies beyond the horizon of physical life, because it has been there, or, to speak more accurately, because even now it has its dwelling place not merely 'in the light of setting suns', but in that mystic day beneath the rim of the world, that day which is night to us because we see only with the eyes of the body. 'That which is Night to all beings, that is Day to the Seer', as the Bhagavad-Gita puts it. Conversely, 'that which is Day to all beings is but Night to the Seer'.

Let us then seek the soul within its cave and ask of it its wisdom.

THE MORTAL: What happens after death?

THE SOUL: *remains silent.*

THE MORTAL: I ask again, what happens after death?

THE SOUL: Who are you who speak?

THE MORTAL: I? I am just a man. My name imports nothing, for I speak on behalf of all my brothers. We who, like gladiators, are about to die, salute thee, Caesar, who art reputed deathless and a God.

THE SOUL: Who is it that dies?

THE MORTAL: This body dies and is no more. There are those among us who hold that with it all is at an end. Earth to earth, air to air; there is no life but what is in the body.

THE SOUL: Yet, when you sleep and dream, your body is unconscious, though you still see and hear, feel joy and pain. Who is this 'you' that sees and hears without the body's help?

THE MORTAL: I know what you would say: that in dream we have experience in a subtle body which also survives death. That is a superstition of the past which arose when men knew nothing of the true nature of dreams, but now we know that they are caused by repressed desires, desires which in our waking life are denied expression.

THE SOUL: You are entangled in a web of words. Do things become different because you give them different names? In those past ages, which you so despise, it was also taught that the dream body was the body of desire, yes, of desires of which the waking ego was not conscious. Have you not heard of *vāsanā*,* the unforgotten longings of the past? Your eyes are blinded by the shadows that you call material things, so that you see no reality save what is physical. I ask again, what is the 'you' who dreams?

THE MORTAL:Whatever it is, it is not 'I' myself, for those desires that find expression in my dreams are those that have been rejected by my personality. They seem to belong to a being that is wider and deeper than my being, one whose memory is greater than my memory, and whose standards and judgements are not my own. Whose are the dreams? Shall I not say those of a great unconscious life in which myself is but a patch of foam, a wave, a passing form that moves upon the sea which gave it birth.

THE SOUL: Even against your will you see the truth, save that you wrongly term that life 'unconscious', because, forsooth, you are not conscious of it. I tell you that nowhere in the universe is there life without consciousness, and nowhere consciousness that is not life. Your personality is indeed a pattern on the surface of that sea, a pattern which by law has come to be, which changes hourly, and in time will cease. It was the winds of desire that brought that wave, that pattern, into being: they speed it on its course, changing it every moment, and only when those winds grow calm and cease, not at what you call death, will it subside once more into the sea. If you believe yourself to be that wave, then you will surely die and be no more, for patterns ever change, giving birth to new. In truth, you die at every moment and not at 'death' alone, since for two moments you are not the same, but change and change for ever. Are you so pleased with the pattern you call yourself that you would have it endure for all eternity?

THE MORTAL: By no means! But I would perfect the pattern and in perfected form enjoy eternal life.

THE SOUL: And you may. But then you must identify yourself with that unchanging being out of which all patterns rise. Moreover, no patterns are perfect in and for themselves, but only the great Pattern of the Whole. I am that Whole, and therefore if you seek

*Vāsanā: The impression of anything remaining unconsciously in the mind.

eternal life, it is in me and not in any finite part that you must live.

THE MORTAL: But I, I, I – it seems that that life you promise me will no longer be myself, that I must go out as the flame of a candle, and my precious uniqueness be lost in something which I cannot feel to be myself.

THE SOUL: If it is self you seek, your precious uniqueness, as you call it, then you are right. Do what you will, that self must change and pass; it cannot stand for ever. But I tell you that the self to which you cling is a source of fear to you, the hard and knotted root of all your sorrow. Why should you cling to what brings naught to you but tears, and why with foolish owl-like eyes do you see only the passing wave and not the water of which the wave is made? Know that you are the water, not the wave, and all your grief is gone – you are immortal.

THE MORTAL: Perhaps. But still your immortality seems cold to me. What of my memory, the record of my joys and griefs, my loves and hates, my struggles and my failures? What is that immortality in which all that has happened to me, all that I have done, is lost? All I have striven for of good, all I have seen of beauty, will be lost as if it had never been.

THE SOUL: Not so, for memory remains in me. Goodness and beauty can exist in me alone, for both are aspects of the one harmonious Whole, not of the warring parts. While you are a self, you catch but fitful glimpses of the wondrous Pattern that is in me. I am the tree of which you are the leaves. I sent you forth and fed you with my sap, to breathe the sunlight and the air of summer. You fall and wither, but the air and light you gathered is not lost. It enters into me and lives on in me, becoming that life-blood with which, after the night of winter, you go forth again.

THE MORTAL: Not so, indeed! It is another leaf that is put forth next year; and so it seems it will not be I who am born again, but someone new, an heir to me, perhaps, but not myself.

THE SOUL: Your self, your self! Can you not lose that self? Have you not heard the ancient saying, 'He who would save his soul shall lose it'? Those words came from one who knew me to the full and therefore was able also to say, 'Heaven and earth shall pass away, but my words shall not pass away'. All who have

known me have known this, and in various words have striven to
teach their fellows. All that is true, good, and beautiful in you
shall live eternally in me, as all that is useful in the food you eat
lives on in you. Why should you seek to keep the worthless dross?

THE MORTAL: Words, words, words! I come to you seeking to know
my fate, and you, like the oracles of the ancient world, put me off
with pictures and riddling words. I do not understand your
waves, your leaves, your food. You will exhaust the universe
with metaphors, and still I do not understand, do not accept your
meaning.

THE SOUL: There you have spoken: you do not *accept* the truth. As
for my words, what would you have of me? I spoke the truth
first in silence, but you heard it not. You would have words, and
what are words but pictures? Even those abstract words of which
you nowadays make so much use are in the end but pictures
taken from your sense experience; and sense experience, as even
you must know, is mortal. How can the mortal reveal the immortal? Yet if you will but use your words as windows, and look
through them, not build them as a wall to hide behind, even
through those words you may behold the wordless truth.

THE MORTAL: Will you not tell me plainly what takes place at death?

THE SOUL: Plainly I told you. Listen now again.

When you were young, there was a life in you that rose within
your being as the sap within a tree. Your body grew, and with it
grew your mind, till, like the summer sun, it reached mid-heaven
and behold the earth spread out before its gaze. King-like it gazed,
warming with its own glory the world of things, and living in that
warmth. But there it could not stay, for all things change, and
that which rises up must fall again. Slowly that ebb set in. The
life that warmed the things again withdrew; your body hardened
and grew cold in its recesses; your mind, though with regret,
retired within itself, turning its back upon the world without,
to live in its own memories, and, were it wise, to seek infinity
within its own cool depths. Is it not so, and is it not for this that
you have come to me in search of knowledge of the land of
death, a land for which you cared but little while the tide of life
flowed outward from your eyes?

THE MORTAL: Your words are true. Say on.

THE SOUL: That life of which I speak, that life which is your Self, sinks down into your heart, until at length your body grows all cold and moves but feebly, answering no more the rudder of your will. Now comes the end; it ceases; it is dead. The mind —

THE MORTAL: What of the mind? Does it not also cease?

THE SOUL: Patience. The mind has turned within itself; it holds no further traffic with the world of outer beings, but lives alone, feeding on its rich store of images and thoughts, as even you would know if you had studied in that hall of learning that you men call dreams. Enter that hall and study now if you would learn the deathlessness of life.

THE MORTAL: You mean that after death the mind is wrapped in dreams? What are those dreams?

THE SOUL: What are all dreams? The tissue of desire, a web which your desires weave from the fibre of your outer life. Your acts in life were motivated by desire; as your desires have been, so shall be now your dreams. Here are those hells, with flames of lust and hatred of which your sacred books told tales to frighten children — true tales, if rightly understood. Here, too, are heavens, heavens of peace and pleasure. But all are transient, passing like shadows, as the stored up energy which called them forth discharges and grows calm.

THE MORTAL: And then?

THE SOUL: 'Ease after toil, port after stormy seas'. Deeper and deeper sinks the life within. The zone of dreams is passed, and the boat of the soul enters on a great calm. It was yourself in life who made those dreams, yes, you who made your heavens and your hells. How long they lasted and of what sort they were was all decided by the course you steered in life. Once you have entered the night that is below the world's horizon, your course is set, the dreams can but unroll. Yet, long or short, happy or sorrowful, they too, like all things finite, have their end, and all is peace.

THE MORTAL: The peace of utter oblivion?

THE SOUL: Oblivion of the forces of desire. Before that peace is entered, the body of desires will die, as dies the outer form that is your body now; and even the desire itself will sleep, as sleeps the life hidden in winter seeds, to wake again in season. Therefore it is that he whose life on earth has been given over entirely to desires can know but little of the nature of the peace, but sleeps in blissful, dark unconsciousness, like dreamless slumber after storm-tossed dreams. He who on earth has raised his head above the turbid waters of desire and sought the vision here of truth and beauty will find no dark unconscious cloud of sleep, but a bright light in which shines forth all he but glimpsed before, 'on earth the broken arcs; in heaven the perfect round'. All men thus come to me, as all men nightly come in dreamless sleep. But though I shelter all within my being, only those who, awake, have seen my face, can know me consciously during the night, whether of sleep or death.

But to all who enter my being is given one flash of light in which, like pictures of the past, unrolling before the mental eye of him who drowns, there comes a vision of the endless thread of life, weaving its pattern on the loom of day and night. All those past days, that flowing stream of lives, endlessly stretching to the very rim of time, shine for a moment as this latest day is added to their number. In their light the mind sees something of the purpose of the whole, and thus of me who am the life in all. Then the veil falls once more; midnight is passed; after the ebb, the flow begins anew. The stream of life, re-energized by contact with its source, flows forth once more to seek the light of day.

THE MORTAL: Then we are born again?

THE SOUL: Rebirth there is, but whether he who is reborn is you is for yourself to judge. The stream of life is one, ebbing and flowing, weaving through many lives, with other streams, the Pattern of the Whole. That stream which was yourself, which, if you like, is still yourself, flows forth, entering the zone of dreams. In that zone, desire awakes once more and fashions for itself a body of desires that is the heir of those it left behind before it entered peace. This is what you call *karma*, others, fate. Guided by those desires, it seeks and finds a human pair who can provide it with a mortal body fitted for its needs, needs judged by *me*, acting as you would say, instinctively within the stream. Thus the life mingles with the two parental streams, enters their hearts and the new-forming body of a child, and so is born to see another day, with an inheritance of countless lives, but with a new body, memory, and brain.

THE MORTAL: So memory is lost? I feared as much.

THE SOUL: Memory remains in me alone, the memory of lives too numerous to count. That memory is yours, if, during life, you learn to enter me. If not, I keep it for you till we meet again once more. Your brain is new, and in it will be stored those memories alone in which it has a part, so that you start 'once more on your adventure brave and new', unburdened by a load of memories too great for you to bear. Yet the stored wisdom of your past is always with you, for it remains in me who am in you. If you will listen for my voice within your heart, that voice will guide you so that in the maze of life your course will be shaped by a wisdom springing from you know not where, a wisdom that is not your own, but mine, and yet which is your Self, for you are me. Thus does the cycle of the nights and days turn on, until the pattern is complete, and pattern blends with pattern in a vast and wondrous whole, too great for you to grasp with finite mind.

And now, farewell; in all things seek for me who am your friend, your life, your very Self. He who finds me sees light within the darkness, life in the midst of death, joy in the heart of sorrow, rest on the wheel of change, love in the midst of hate.

THE MORTAL: Tell me, then, who thou art; where shall I find thee?

THE SOUL: Who or what I am cannot be told. Words may describe yourself, but never me who am beyond their grasp. As for the Path by which I may be found, I speak: it is for you to seize my meaning.

Seek me in the dark cave within your heart. There in the night that is the heart of day, seek out the day that is the heart of night. Hear without ears, and see without your eyes; then, in the hidden depths you will behold an altar, floating in the air without support. On it there shines a flame that burns without wick or fuel. Enter that flame and, although Self must die, find me.

5. *Doubts and Their Removal*

People in general have a very wrong attitude towards doubt. Instead of regarding doubt as the pathway to knowledge, they consider it as something wrong, something that should never have occurred. Doubt is the doorway to knowledge, and this is the reason why science, which relies on doubts and experiment, has made such progress, while religion, which relies on the blind acceptance of what was written in books hundreds or thousands of years ago, is gradually losing its hold on men's hearts. All the knowledge that we have is the result of someone's having doubted something that most people of the time believed to be true. And this is as true in the field of religion as in that of science.

What is religion nowadays? For the most part it consists in accepting blindly a set of beliefs taught by one's father or teachers. One hears men say: 'My religion says so and so; our community says so and so; our sacred books say so and so.' As if it mattered a pin what one's religion says, what one's community believes, or what one's sacred books teach! The one thing that matters is the Truth; and Truth is only to be attained by caring nothing for what one's community or one's books say, and by fearlessly pursuing it with one's heart and soul, caring for nothing until it is attained.

It does not matter in the least how many beliefs have to be abandoned, how many illusions vanish on the way. The Truth stands forever, and those who are afraid of the path of free enquiry that leads to it will never reach the goal. Just as an honest man fears no enquiry into his actions, so he who seeks the Truth fears no enquiry into the grounds of his beliefs, for he knows that what is true can never be shaken, while whatever can be shaken by free enquiry is not the truth and can have no real value.

Genuine doubts must not be confused with the senseless habit of arguing for the sake of arguing, or for the sake of displaying one's own learning. Nor, again, must doubt about ultimate questions lead to refusal to come to a conclusion on any matter at all. For instance, the fact that one has not been able to understand the origin of the world must not lead one to refuse assent to what can be shown to be true, any more than a scientist's inability to understand the ultimate nature of electricity leads him to doubt that an electric motor works.

Sincere doubts, however, are the first signs of progress. If a pupil has doubts, his teacher should not consider it a sign of wickedness, but should encourage him, for they are a sign that he has been thinking for himself, and to think for oneself is the first stage on the path to Truth.

Having got so far, it will not stop there. The mind must not be allowed to remain in doubt permanently, for that weakens the mind and kills all action and progress. Once a doubt has arisen in one's mind, every effort must be made to answer it properly. Usually what people do is to silence it, to thrust it out of sight, and to pretend that it does not exist. This, however, is of no use. The doubt is thrust into the inner recesses of the heart, and there it continues to live and to poison the mind of the doubter, like a hidden abscess in the body. In order to silence the doubting voice in his heart, the doubter proclaims his opinions outwardly with more and more vehemence, and, just because in his heart he does not believe them, he seeks to convert others to them that he may gain support through feeling that many are on his side. Suppressed doubt is thus the source of most religious propaganda, and it is usually true that he who is most urgent to convert others to his religion or point of view is he who feels most doubts in his own heart. This is the path of fanaticism and hypocrisy, so he who has come to feel a doubt about something or other should spare no efforts to solve it.

The first step is to make sure that one has understood the problem correctly, and for that purpose it is useful to listen to what competent people have to say on the subject, to read what has been written about it in books.

This, however, is only the first step, and if the answer is not found, then one must prepare to find it for oneself. For this purpose two things are necessary: perfect mental sincerity and untiring efforts.

We must not allow our prejudices and desires to interfere with our enquiry. We must honestly face all the facts and not hide them with the idea that, if we just shut our eyes to facts, they themselves cease to exist.

Next comes effort. Having understood exactly what the problem is, we must bend all our efforts towards its solution, as a starving man bends all his efforts towards finding food. All day the problem must occupy our thoughts. Not only in hours of meditation, but at all times we must think and think, and then, having done so, hold the mind quiet so that, if possible, the answer may come. When the tension in the mind has become sufficient, it is quite certain that an answer will come, and, if it does not, it only means either that sufficient thinking has not been done, or else that the question has not been rightly put. It is no use trying to solve a question of which the various terms have not been understood. For instance, it is no good asking why God made the world, until you are entirely clear as to what the word 'God' means to you. Only when all the terms are clear can an answer possibly come.

If, however, you are certain that you understand all the terms in the question and still an answer does not come, you must think again and again until the tension is sufficient. Then, one day, either as a flash of insight when the mind is stilled, or as a dream when stilled in sleep, the answer will come.

But do not think, because you have had a dream or a vision during meditation, that therefore this is certainly the truth and the God has revealed it to you. Dreams and visions can be utterly misleading. You must examine the answer carefully and see if it satisfies your reason and heart. If it does not, then you will have to start all over again. If it does satisfy you, then you have found your answer; even so, you must not assume that it represents the final truth. Very likely you are not ready yet to understand the full truth, and so have received the truest answer that you could understand. Therefore you should always be ready to modify what you had previously thought to be true in the light of further knowledge, just as a scientist is always ready to abandon past theories in the light of new facts.

Thus it can be seen that the Path to Truth is a laborious, uphill one. Mistake after mistake will be made, but if you persist untiringly and never give up hope, then, sooner or later, you will reach that knowledge which 'being known, all else is known'. This is the only safe and certain path. Other ways will either leave you stranded in the sterile desert of orthodoxy, or else lost in the jungle of illusion. Opinions you can pick up anywhere, but if you want the Truth, you will have to tread this path, however hard. Of this, however, you may be certain, namely, that sincerity and effort will inevitably bring you success in the end.

In yourself the Truth exists. By yourself it must be striven for and tested. In yourself it will be found.

6. *Past, Present and Future*

One of the significant features of the age in which we live is the peculiar intensification of interest in the future and the constant efforts that are being made to predict its course. We are not referring here to the very widespread revival of interest in the ancient science of astrology, though that, too, is symptomatic, but to the ever increasing spate of books and articles dealing with expected new developments that are thought to be hanging about somewhere just round the corner, to the universally prevalent discussions of the science of the future, the religion of tomorrow, the art of the new age, and the coming social system.

When we find that a great deal of our psychic energy is thus going into the task of speculating about the future, we can be sure that 'something is rotten in the state of Denmark', that is to say, in our own psyche at the present moment, that there is in fact some present situation with which we are not dealing adequately. It may be said that, when the world around us is in the deplorable state in which it presently is, it is 'quite natural' that we should cast longing eyes on the future.

In truth, the answer to no real problem can ever be found in the outer world, for it does not exist there, but in the psyche. The so-called outer world, the environment which seems to surround us, is a projection of our inner psychic states, as certainly as the picture on the screen is the projection of the slide in the magic-lantern. However much common sense, which is merely the advocate paid to argue for the continuance of the present conditions, may protect against this statement, it nevertheless represents a plain fact, though admittedly one which it is not easy for us to realize at all fully. At least we can easily recognize and make a starting point from one fact, namely, that the 'same' environment, as common sense counts sameness, is a different thing in different psychic conditions. To one man a jungle, far removed from the haunts of men, is a place of infinite peace, beauty, and satisfaction. To another, or even to the same man in a different psychic state, it is a place of intense fear or boredom. The same is true of any other environment we may select, an office, a laboratory, or a garden-party. We see that we have projected from ourselves; the actual screen is neutral.

But besides this projection on to the immediate environment, this spatialization of our psychic contents, there is also another type: a projection into time. The former gives rise to an interest in the world around us which therefore shines with a light of attraction or repulsion that is quite foreign to its nature, being, in fact, derived from ourselves. The latter gives rise to an interest in past or future which, too, shines with a light that is derived from us, a light that is of an entirely magical nature. This has been noticed even by materialists, for we find Bertrand Russell saying: 'This is why the past possesses such a magical power'. Like Duncan, 'after life's fitful fever it sleeps well', revealing words to any who can see their meaning. We may note also the aura of magic light that Keats throws round his poem 'St Agnes' Eve' by the words of the concluding verse –

> And they are gone, ay, ages long ago
> These lovers fled away into the storm.

As these words are pronounced, a change comes over the mood of the reader. A spell has been uttered, and instantly the whole story with its rich texture of fearless, danger-laden passion is immobilized by a wave of the enchanter's wand and removed into the safety of 'ages long ago'.

What, then, is the present, what the past and future? We shall here use our writer's privilege of stating facts without argument, and we shall do so the more readily because such facts as these are either seen or not seen; no arguments can convince him who will not see, and there are only too many reasons why we should fear to face the truth.

The present, that environment which surrounds us as we write or read these words and which seems so real, so solid, and so shin-breaking, is the projection of all in the psyche that is clear and overt, all that of which, whether liked or disliked, we are clearly conscious; and it fades away into a horizon background, a penumbra, in which, though not clearly conscious at the moment, is all that can become conscious of by a simple change of viewpoint.

The past is the region into which we project all that we fear within ourselves, all that we wish to render powerless by the double technique of forgetfulness and immobilization. The terrible demons that stalk the Soul, lords of blood and ruthless lust from which we need protection, are thus removed from us by the un-consciously uttered magic spell which places them securely in the past. This is the reason why what is known as history, especially ancient history, is so bloody and terrible. What else could it be when we have used its blank, imaginary pages for drawing pictures of our own most desperate fears, all that we have deliberately forgotten because we dare not face its present power?

The future on the other hand, is the region into which we project all that we desire, all those psychic states we should like to be conscious of, but dare not face because of their incompatibility with all that we are used to. To accept these shining Gods as present realities, which indeed they are, would mean altering so much to which we are habituated that we prefer to remove them into the magic twilight of the future. Were the longed-for new age to be born now (which it could be, would we but face it, for it is an eternal present) it would mean the upsetting of too many cher-ished habits of thought and feeling. It is therefore safer to push it away around the corner, and thus place it in a state where it can be 'desired' without our having to alter our present psychic structures and habits.

The future need not be immobilized as we immobilize our fears into the static eternity of the past, for, although fear is only the negative shadow, the female counterpart of desire, the future is those elements which are 'desired' not 'feared'. The future is thus allowed to be a 'living' region: all that is required of it is that it shall remain sufficiently vague to avoid its present implications being clearly seen. The past, because immobilized, can be allowed to be clearly seen, at least in parts: the future must be dim and only twilit.

It will be objected that many people fear the dark future and look with longing love upon the golden past. This, though true, is not an objection. Our psychic magic is not and cannot be absolute. Those lords of terror whom we have established in the past are, it is true, reduced to immobility; their dread forms are prevented from approaching us; but our magic extends no further than what we may term their bodies. Their souls are free of it, and, leaping over the present, haunt the future in the dim mist of which their moving shadows are dimly descried, advancing, like all future, upon us with awful gestures that threaten vengeance for all the spells laid on their bodies. It is a perception of these dim but ominous shapes, moving amidst the clouds of things to come, that cause that future land of heart's desire to be, to some, a terror more dreadful, even, than the past.

Similarly, while the bright Gods of desire are allowed to move in their land of the future, though with their lustre dimmed by its twilight mists, *their* souls are shining beacons, golden pillars in the ever-standing past, and lend to the latter the magic light by which it so fascinates the soul. Thus do all things pass into their opposites.

As we thus gaze, the whole of time comes rushing in upon us, and the entire universe concentrates to a point. Against that centring flood the mental personality, or ego, in whose interests and for whose protection the great panorama of space and time is maintained, protests and marshals all its defences. The first defence is plain denial of the facts, a passionate reaffirmation of the entire reality of the past, present, and future. Nevertheless, what we have stated is true, a truth not of our childish, ego-protecting logic, but one which can be seen by those bold enough to open their eyes and gaze, by those convinced that to lose the ego-life is to find true being. For such, the tyranny of time and space is ended. The living ramparts of the universe sweep in on rushing wings until their concentrated power ignites a spark of infinite intensity: such is the birth of an eternal star, a guide to those who wander in the night.*

*This is the meaning of the tremendous *janmādyasya* of the *Brahma Sūtras*, for it is out of that infinite intension of the soul or *Ātman* that has arisen the past of birth, in it that stands the wide-extended plain of present maintenance, and from it that rushes on us the dark future of death and change. *Nāgārjuna* has told us that 'The entire sphere of phenomena dissolves with the dissolution of the protective sphere of thought'.

The same truth has been expressed by the great Gaudapāda: 'The birthlessness of Mind thus free from the notion of causality is unconditioned and absolute. All is forever unborn, for all is objectivization of the mind . . . Not finding any objective cause, one easily reaches that which is ever free from sorrow, desire, and fear [i.e. *from present, future and past time*]. The Changeless State is reached when the mind frees itself from duality and self-objectivization. This is indeed the Field of the Wise, the Unconditioned, the Unborn, the One. The childish miss it by predicating of it such things as existence, non-existence, both together, or neither . . . but he has seen all who has seen the Glorious Being, untouched by any of the predicates which serve only to hide it from the seer.' (*Māndūkya Kārika*, 77 *et seq.*)

7. Superstition

The *Īshopanishad* mentions two movements of thought which it terms *Vidyā* and *Avidyā*, respectively. Surprisingly enough to many, it affirms that an exclusive clinging to *either* of these two modes lands us in deep darkness. 'Into blind darkness go they who cling to *Avidyā* alone; but into an even greater darkness, as it were, go they who cling to *Vidyā* alone.'

It is not intended to enter on a discussion of the root meaning of these two terms, conventionally translated as knowledge and ignorance, but to point out that one among the many pairs of opposites in which they manifest is a pair we may describe as superstition and (merely rational) enlightenment.

Let us take an example at random from the countless beliefs that constitute the web of religion. Hindus hold that bathing in the Gangā purifies from sin, and are therefore given to the habit of regular ceremonial bathings, particularly at specially holy centres such as Benares. While such ritual bathing is quite universal among the orthodox, few, when asked, can give any rational explanation of the efficacy of the rite, but are content to say that it has been taught in the scriptures and therefore should be performed. Such performance of a rite without knowledge of its meaning may be termed superstition, a mode of *Avidyā*, and undoubtedly the superstitious man remains in darkness.

Over against such an attitude of blind acceptance of what has been taught arises another, one which may also be found within the Hindu fold, but which is more markedly present among the more rationalistic Buddhists who, indeed, are in the habit of referring to Hindus as *tīrthikas* or 'bathers'. This second attitude consists in subjecting the practice in question to the fire of an ethico-intellectual criticism, and in rejecting it because of its apparent inability to satisfy such ethico-intellectual canons.

Thus, with regard to this practice of bathing in the Gangā, such critics will point out that physical entities, like water, cannot interact with moral entities, like sin, that if Gangā water purified from sin, then fishes and crocodiles would be purified by living in it, that there is no evidence to show that such purification is actually brought about, and, finally, that it is a mischievous doctrine, leading people to go on sinning in the fancied security of being able to wash it away with another bath.

This is the mode of merely rational enlightenment, a mode of *Vidyā*, and it leads to 'even greater darkness'. The Upanishad goes on to tell that the two modes must be united: 'by *Avidyā* crossing over death, by *Vidyā* deathlessness is attained'.

Before attempting to see how this synthesis or fusion of opposites is to be achieved, we may note two false approaches. The first is what may be termed the 'electric' or 'pseudo-scientific'. For instance, many years ago doctors discovered that Gangā water contained small creatures that they portentously termed bacteriophagi, creatures which have the useful property of eating up disease germs and so keeping the water fresh and wholesome. This fact was no doubt known to 'our ancient Rishis' who therefore taught the religious efficacy of bathing in the Gangā. The bacteriophagi are a fact; their connection with psychic or spiritual purification is not obvious.

The second method is even worse. It consists in keeping the two modes in water-tight compartments. The 'rational' criticism is adopted, in fact it is even paraded, but the 'superstitious' practice is kept on all the same, in order 'to please the women-folk'. The first method is a real attempt, though a confused one, at reconciliation: the second disrupts the unity of the psyche, thus destroying sincerity. Before we go any further, however, let us first see if, apart from the Upanishadic statement, there is any harm in not attempting a synthesis at all.

Why not go on with the 'superstition', continue to bathe in the Gangā in 'simple faith', without worrying about the rationalist criticism? That is all right so long as the rational criticism has not come to our ears or made itself felt by us. Once its voice has penetrated to our consciousness, it is impossible for the 'simple faith' to continue as before. We can forcibly shut out or repress the voice, but it will be there in our hearts all the same, and psychic unity and its resultant sincerity will be destroyed. Once having heard, we cannot un-hear. We must answer.

Well then, why not accept the criticism and give up the 'superstition' altogether? This is what is often done by people of what may be termed the protestant type of mind. The results, however, are quite peculiarly disastrous, for what is literally a spiritual blindness sets in which leaves the world darker than any darkness of superstition. Moreover, the blindness is apt to set in so gradually that, by the time it is complete, we forget that we ever had powers of vision, that a state of light ever existed. For it is not just one 'superstition' that is involved, but a whole way of life, and the result is that the whole world is emptied of Gods. From earth and water, from air and fire, the Gods takes flight. Nothing divine is left anywhere, and even the sun himself becomes to our vision a mere ball of burning gas, spluttering away above us in an empty sky. Divinity is chased away to some remote heaven beyond all possibility of that sacramental contact which alone can give significance to life. Who but a beast would care to dwell in a world which all the Gods have left?

Let us then return to the starting point and see if the disastrous antinomy cannot be avoided there. By bathing in the Gangā we are purified from sin. How can merely material water purify us from psychic sin? But is water 'merely material'? Is there any such thing as 'merely material'? Are not all things the dwelling place of Spirit? Surely we must admit that when we bathe we are refreshed in Spirit, and such refreshment is a psychic experience which could not be brought about by 'mere matter'.

The truth is that Gangā is not just a stream of water but an embodied Spirit born from the feet of Nārāyana, the dweller in the waters. We do not dispute the truth, as far as they go, of the mapmakers' statements about the source of all that they can see and mark on a map, the source of what they know of the river Ganges, but such statements are only partial. The real source of a book is to be found in the author's mind: the printer's account of it in terms of cloth, paper, and ink, is only external. A book is a spirit, dwelling in the form of ink and paper: by plunging into it we can be transported out of ourselves, surely an astonishing result to be caused by 'mere' black marks on white paper! If the heart can be purified by plunging into the pages of a book, why can it not be purified by plunging in the waters of a river? Such purification, however, depends on whether we can 'read' what is written on the paper or what is written in the waters, in other words, upon whether we can use the material form as a means of establishing contact with the mind of its author. The author in both cases is Spirit, and, just as the spirit of a man dwells in the pages of a book, so does the Spirit of God dwell in the waters of a river. If the former can purify and elevate our hearts, so undoubtedly can the latter.

Purusha and *Prakriti* (Spirit and Matter) are forever blended in the tissue of the world. Nowhere is there anything which is Matter alone, nor is there anything which is Spirit alone. He who seeks only Matter sees only Matter anywhere; for him all things are dead and powerless. He who seeks also the living Spirit sees Spirit in all things, 'all things are full of Gods'; all things are living powers; all things have their effect upon the living Spirit of man.

But why Gangā particularly? This is a question that is sure to be asked: why not any stream? There is a proverb to the effect that for him whose heart is strong, a tub of water can serve as Gangā. Nevertheless, all hearts are not equally strong, and therefore all ancient peoples, all those who lived in the same world as Gods, selected one or more rivers (just as they selected one or more books as 'scriptures') on account of their grandeur, fertilizing power, or central position, to be, *par excellence*, their sacred waters. Such, among many others, were the Hindu Gangā, the Egyptian Nile, and the Jewish Jordan. Nevertheless, it is well known that in the Himalayas all streams are called Gangā.

Perhaps it will be said that all this is very well for subtlety-spinning philosophers: what about the simple folk who reck little of *Purusha* and *Prakriti* and to whom the river is just a river? We reply that the sophisticated sceptic knows little and understands nothing of what is passing in the hearts of the simple and inarticulate. Much is known to the heart that cannot be expressed, much that is almost entirely forgotten in the course of an education which

102 Initiation into Yoga

concerns itself with learning to express quite other things. One thing is certain, namely, that to the simple-hearted a river is most emphatically *not* 'just a river'.

We cannot conclude better than with the words of the same Upanishad:

> My life-breath to the immortal Wind of Spirit;
> My body ends in ashes.

Yet life is found in the embrace of both: that which affects the one, affects the other. The golden serpent of eternity has its own tail within its mouth.

8. The Violence of War

Wars are psychic events that have their birth in the souls of men. We like to put the blame for them upon the shoulders of our favourite scapegoat, upon imperialism, nationalism, communism, or capitalism, whichever be our chosen bogey. Not any or all of these are really responsible, but we ourselves, we harmless folk who like to think that we hate war and all its attendant horrors. We may have had no finger in the muddy waters of politics or finance, we may have written no articles or even letters tending to inflame national, racial, or communal passions, yet we are all sharers in the responsibility.

Every feeling of anger, hatred, envy, and revenge that we have indulged in the past years, no matter whom it was directed against and however 'justified' it may seem to us to have been, has been a handful of gunpowder thrown on to the pile which must, sooner or later, explode as now it has done.

But it is not he or they who struck the match that is or are responsible for a world in flames, but we who helped to swell the pile of powder. For what is it that we have done? The states of hatred, fear, etc, that have entered our hearts and there met with indulgence are, as always, intolerable guests. We hasten to project them outside ourselves, to affix them like posters upon any convenient wall. Doubtless there was something in the nature of the wall that made it a suitable vehicle for that particular poster, but, all the same, the poster came from us and was by us affixed.

Whether we look at the psychology of individuals, or at those aggregates of individuals which we call national states, the process is the same. That which we hate or fear in ourselves we project upon our neighbours. He who fears his own sex desires discerns impurity in all whom he meets; in the same way, nations that are filled with hatred, fear, and aggressive desire perceive the images of those passions burning luridly upon the ramparts of other nations, not realizing that it is they themselves who have lit and placed them there. Thus arises the myth of the peace-loving nations and individuals, just because we project our own aggressive desires upon our neighbours and thus secure the illusion of personal cleanliness.

This is not to say that the responsibility of all nations is alike, any more than is that of all individuals. Some of us have sinned more deeply than others, but the assessment of such responsibility is never easy. It is more important and also profitable for us to remember that all hatred, fear, envy, and aggressive desire, by whomsoever and however 'privately' entertained, has been the fuel which prepared and still maintains the blaze. Every time we feel a thrill of triumph at the destruction of 'the enemy', we add to it, for each time we do so we are making others the scapegoats for the evil in ourselves. This is not mere philosophic talk; it is not even religion; it is sheer practical fact which any psychologist will confirm.

None of us, not the most determined conscientious objector, not the most isolationist of neutrals, can escape his share of responsibility. Indeed, it is often just those who do not partake in the actual physical fighting who do most with their thoughts to increase the conflict. Fighting men, after a few months of experience have been gained, are often to a surprising degree free from hatred, while those who sit in comfortable isolation only too frequently indulge their own baser excitements and passions by exulting in vicarious horrors, making a cinema show out of the agonies of others, fighting to the last drop of (others') blood, and fanning the flames of hatred and violence with the unseen wind of their own thoughts and feelings.

For there is that in all men which welcomes war; yes, welcomes it even to the point of willingness to undergo its sufferings. In almost all men there is much that social and religious convention will not in normal times permit to find expression. There is a caged beast in the hearts of most of us, a beast whose substance we should like to gratify, but cannot for fear of consequences. Usually he nourishes his subterranean life on the scraps of phantasy and daydream that filter down to the den where he sits, brooding on deeds of violence and cruelty by which he may be revenged for his confinement; and each time we indulge in phantasies of hatred or revenge those thoughts sink down and add to his ferocious energy. Sometimes we can feel him straining against the confining bars, but in normal times 'God' and the policemen keep him down, so that only occasionally does he escape and the world is shocked by some deed of atrocious cruelty. When this occurs, society decides that that man's cage is too weak to hold its beast, and, fearing the example on others if one should be allowed to escape with impunity, hurriedly proceeds to destroy both man and beast.

It is necessary to add that the beast is not destroyed by the killing of the body which was its cage. Unseen by men it roams about, freed of its cage of flesh, free also to enter in the heart of any man who will give it temporary shelter and to urge him to the vile deeds that it loves. If men in general became aware of the extent to which this happens, they would not be so eager to kill those who commit ghastly crimes – nor their personal enemies either.

This is what happens in normal times. But in times of war all is different. 'Cry havoc and let loose the dogs of war' is no mere poetic metaphor. The hell-hounds from within *are* loosed. All that was 'sinful' and forbidden before is now encouraged in the service of the State. Hatred, violence, ferocity, cruelty, as well as every variety of deceitful cunning, all these become virtues in those who direct them against 'the enemy'. Even those whose States are not at war feel the contagion and, taking sides in the struggle, indulge their beasts in imagination.

Thus do the periods of war and peace succeed one another through the weary centuries of history. It is not intended to deny that in certain circumstances the open and outer violence of armed resistance may not be the lesser of two evils, for in the present state of humanity the alternative is too often a violence of thought and feeling, an obsessive brooding over hatred and revenge that is far worse than outward fighting. But never will violence bring violence to an end. As long as we nourish the brutes within our hearts with the desire-laden thoughts that are their life-blood, so long will they break out from time to time, and so long will periodical wars be inevitable.

The only way to real peace is the taming of those inner beasts. We who have created them, bone of our bone and flesh of our flesh, must weaken them by giving them no food, must re-absorb them into our conscious selves from which in horror we have banished them, and finally must transmute their very substance by the alchemy of spirit. And that is yoga: only in yoga is peace.

'The world is just one's thought; with effort then it should be cleansed by each one of us. As is one's thought, so one becomes; this is the eternal secret.'* Those who care for peace and hate war must keep more vigilant guard over their thoughts and phantasies than in normal times. Every exulting thought at news of the destruction of the 'enemy' (as though man had any enemy but the one in his own bosom), every indulgence in depression at 'our own' disasters, every throb of excitement at the deeds of war in general is a betrayal of humanity's cause. Those who enjoy a physical isolation from the fighting are in possession of an opportunity that is a sacred trust. If they fail to make use of it to bring about peace in that part of the world-psyche with which they are in actual contact, namely, their own hearts, above all, if they actively misuse that opportunity by loosing their beasts in sympathetic phantasy, then they are secret traitors to humanity. As such, they will be caught within the web of *karma* that they are spinning, a web that will unerringly bring it about that, in the next conflict that breaks out, it will be on them that the great burden of suffering will fall. Of all such it may be said that he who takes the sword in thought and phantasy shall perish by the sword in actual fact.

This is the great responsibility that falls upon all, and especially upon all who by their remoteness from the physical struggle are given the opportunity of wrestling with their passions in some degree of detachment, and so actually lessening the flames of hatred and evil in this world. None can escape, for all life is one. As soon should the little finger think to escape the burning fever which has gripped the body, as any to escape the interlinkedness of all life. Neutral or conscientious objector, householder or world-renouncing *sannyāsi*, none can escape his share of responsibility for a state of things that his own thoughts have helped to bring about; for

Maitri Upanishad.

neither geographical remoteness, nor governmental decree of neutrality, nor yet personal refusal to bear arms can isolate the part from the whole in which it is rooted.

It is in the inner worlds of desire that wars originate, and from those inner worlds that they are maintained. What we see as wars upon this physical plane are but the shadows of those inner struggles, a ghastly phantom show, bodying forth events that have already taken place in the inner world, dead ash marking the destructive path of the forest fire, the troubled and unalterable wake of a ship whose prow is cleaving the waters far ahead. In war or peace we live in a world of shadows cast by events that we term 'future', because, unseen by us as they really happen, we only know them when we come across their wake upon this plane.

Sri Krishna's words, pronounced before the Kurukshetra battle, 'by Me *already* have they all been slain', refer not to any remorseless, divine pre-destination, but to this very fact, and they are as true of those whose bodies will perish in the coming year as they were of those who fought in that war of long ago.

Until we understand and face this basic fact, wars are inevitable, and, struggling in the wake of troubled waters that ourselves have made, fighting with shadows that ourselves have cast, we shall continue to cry out against a hostile and malignant Fate, or if of a more submissive nature, to pray to God to save us from its grip. But prayers and outcries alike are useless: 'Not in the middle regions of the air, nor in the ocean depths; not in the mountain caves, nor anywhere on earth is there a spot where man can escape the fruit of his evil deeds.' In the inner worlds we have made war: in those same inner worlds we must make peace, for 'Mind is the forerunner of all things; by mind are all things made. He who with desire-polluted mind thinks or acts evil, him sorrow follows as the wheel the foot of the ox.'*

*Dhammapada.

9. Religion and Philosophy

Philosophy is a word which formerly had a much wider significance than it now has, and included, under the heading 'Natural Philosophy', all of what we now call science. Gradually, however, the term has become limited to speculative reasoning about the ultimate nature of the universe in its various aspects. It is true that a follower of Hegel would give a different answer to the question, 'What is philosophy?' from that which will be given by, say, Bertrand Russell, but in a general way we may say that philosophy means, in Europe, speculative reasoning about the universe either on a basis of accepted principles *a priori* held to be valid, or on a basis of observed facts, and is an attempt to arrive at an understanding of the universe through the use of the discursive reason.

The classical systems of Indian philosophy start on a different basis altogether. The Sanskrit word usually translated as 'philosophy' is '*darshanam*', which literally means 'seeing', and the Indian systems start neither from *a priori* principles nor from the observed facts, as usually understood, but from some transcendental experience in which the truth about the nature of the universe is directly perceived. What is usually called the 'philosophy' is an attempt to give a coherent and logical account of the world, as thus perceived, in terms that will be both intelligible and convincing to a given hearer. It is a rational demonstration of the truth seen by the original *rishi* or 'seer', and with it is taught a practical method by which the pupil may acquire a realization of the truths demonstrated.

It is this claim to direct experience on the part of the teacher and to the possibility of such for the pupil that makes the widest gulf between the Indian and European systems. In the latter no hope is held out that the pupil will ever arrive at more than an understanding of the truth. Whether one believes with Berkeley that a spade is an idea in the mind of God, or with McTaggart that it is a colony of souls, the practical result is the same as if one believed with the crassest realist that it is just a spade. Whereas, when the author of the Bhagavad-Gita says that 'all is *Vāsudeva*', the indwelling Spirit, he is saying something that he means his hearers to verify for themselves and on which they will be able to base their whole lives and practical outlook on the world.

In the ancient world there was no divorce between philosophy and religion. Religion found its culmination in philosophy, and the latter drove down deep roots into religion. Between the two there was constant communication so that philosophers could expound religious truths to the common man, and the latter could look up to the former as to one who saw clearly the truths that for most were shrouded in symbolism. This was true even in Europe where such men as Plato and Plotinus were not ashamed to speak of the Gods and, though there was much in contemporary religion that they disapproved of, much that was superstitious and must be disapproved of by any man of knowledge, their philosophy was rooted in religion just as much as was that of Shankarāchārya in India. Nor was this fact at all detrimental to their philosophy, for so eminent a modern philosopher as Whitehead has stated that the whole of European philosophy may be described as a series of footnotes to Plato, a remark which shows how true and lasting was the latter's philosophic thought.

In India we have only to think of such great names as Shankarāchārya, Nāgārjuna, Vasubhandhu and Rāmānuja to realize how intimate the connection between religion and philosophy has been in this country, for all these men were both great religious teachers and great philosophers. In later times in the West and in that part of India that takes its cue from the West, all this has been changed – one can hardly think for the better. Philosophy divorced from religion has become a mass of epistemological technicalities, while religion, cut off from philosophy, becomes for the most part an unappetizing mixture of infantilism and superstition. This tendency is spreading gradually even in India, and nowadays many people seem to feel that the proper way to write philosophy is to bring out a learned and technical monograph on the *Vaibhāshika* theory of perception or the *Dwait-ādwaita* view of inference. Of course these topics are, like any other, legitimate playthings for academic specialists, but those who seek from philosophy knowledge of 'that which having known, all else is known' will no more find it in these unprofitable verbal subtleties than they will find it in the empty rituals, the blind dogmatics, and the infantile emotionalism of orthodox religion. That philosophy should become a purely academic pursuit is bad enough. It is infinitely worse that religion should be the happy hunting ground of tearful hysterics, of eloquent gas bags, and of neurotic persons with mother fixations. We have even seen people haunting the steps of a '*mahātma*' who was literally a babbling idiot, in the hope that some of his senseless prattling might reveal the hiding place of buried treasure.

All these extravagances come from the neglect of philosophy which, with its pure mountain air, disperses all the fogs of folly and superstition and summons us to a bracing effort to find the truth for, by, and in ourselves. But the philosophy which can do this must be a real philosophy and not the verbal cobwebs of the schools, for the latter remain elegant constructions. For what will it profit a man to be able to prove in words that reality is composed of ideas, or tables and chairs are colonies of souls, when the mind which has the ideas is as obstinately uncontrollable as ever, the tables and chairs as resolutely inert as those of any materialist?

For God's sake let us get away from words and plunge into the heart's deep core, the well at the bottom of which, as old symbolism tells, Truth lies buried. It is only when philosophy comes from the heart that it will appeal to the heart; all else is but words, 'a tale, told by an idiot, full of sound and fury, signifying nothing'.

We hope to close the chasm which at present is widening between religion and philosophy. How far we shall be able to do so will depend on our contributions; but it is felt that, if it can be done at all, it will be here in India where the great tradition is not yet altogether dead.

Philosophy, if it is to be real love of wisdom and not mere epistemological hair-splitting, must not divorce itself from the practical and emotional discipline of life that constitutes the heart of religion. But that is not enough in itself. If philosophy is not to stultify itself, it must make strenuous efforts to keep free from the only too common systems of rationalized beliefs, fashioned to support this or that socio-political system.

All around us we find philosophy being pressed into the service of political and religious creeds. There is one characteristic common to all these creeds. Their adherents, whether communists, fascists, imperialists, or even ordinary religious believers (wherever and whenever organized religion has any real power), are all and always ready to do violence to the minds and bodies of other people in order to compel their adherence. The free play of the mind, its very life-blood, is offered up in sacrifice to the local Moloch, and it makes no difference at all whether they call that Moloch the great god Stalin, the great god Hitler, the great god Mao Tse Tung, or the great god of orthodox religion. The result is just the same.

Violence is always the same, and he who wishes to be a philosopher must renounce violence of every sort, once and for all. By suitably curving and distorting a mirror, it is possible to make it reflect points that are widely separated in space as though they were close together, and vice versa; but all that has been achieved is a distorted and false reflection that is useless as a guide to reality. The actual facts are not altered.

Similarly, by allowing play to the subterranean forces of desire, it is possible and, indeed, only too easy to distort the mirror of the mind so that things which are not true appear as if they were. This happens whenever we use the intellect to 'prove' the truth of some proposition, when the plain fact is that we merely wish to believe it true. It is always possible to prove to our own apparent satisfaction that it is right that individual welfare and, indeed, all human values should be sacrificed to the deified nation or to some theoretically divine social system, but such 'proofs', attained by doing violence to the mind, always carry with them a compensating disbelief, a sort of inverted image buried deep beneath the shining surface of the mental mirror. Hence the violence with which men are ready to impose their beliefs on others; a cold inverted image of the moon, like the face of a drowned man, is forever dancing mockingly beneath the waves of their hearts.

The idea that violence can bring about a solution of any problem is thoroughly unphilosophical, and yet, behind so many of the thought systems of the world, idealistic, materialistic, or religious, lies the appeal to violence, potential if not actual, mental if not physical. And so we get the spectacle of men of different nations all ready to kill and maim each other in defence of their own unique interests, and all forgetting that the web of life is one and universal. To defend our own women and children against the foreign devil becomes a sacred duty, one which is best performed by inflicting on the enemy's women and children just those abominations that we find so monstrously inhuman when practised on our own.

For the philosopher there should be no such ridiculous mental astigmatism. What is true in one direction is also true in the other. A philosopher who cannot rise above the limitations of the particular viewpoint at which he finds himself by birth is no philosopher at all. His study has been in vain, if it has not given him the power to judge the truth of a belief, to estimate the rightness of an action, irrespective of whether that belief or that action are or are not calculated to bring immediate benefit to 'his' country, the country in which he happened to be born.

Sinister attempts are made to destroy all freedom of thought and to force the minds of men into predetermined channels. Such attempts are bound to fail because the human psyche will not suffer violence and strain indefinitely. Within all hearts is the free and deathless *Ātman*, resistless like the ocean against which men build their puny dams in vain. The *Ātman* works through the hearts and brains of such men as offer themselves in its service. One of the most sacred duties that is laid upon us at this present epoch is to preserve such freedom of thought as we have inherited from those who have gone before, to strive our hardest to enlarge its boundaries, and to resist unswervingly all attempts to destroy the most precious jewel in the world, the freedom and 'the power of man's unconquerable mind'.

Accounts of Hindu–Muslim strife and bloodshed are depressing reading for all who believe that the true function of religion is to bring unity to men and not strife. It is true that many other motives than purely religious ones are always involved in such conflicts, but all history shows that nothing can give a sharper edge to the baser passions of humanity than the stupid belief that they are being

sanctified in the service of some god. There is no cruelty more re-
morselessly inhuman than that of the fanatical priest, and no stupidity more gross than that of the ignorant believer. It is no wonder
that many have urged the abolition of all religion as a prime source
of human suffering.

But religion cannot be abolished. It springs from a source deep
in the human heart, and, if it is destroyed in one form, it immediately rises up again in another. Russian communism and German
Nazism proclaimed war on Christianity, but, is doing so, they have
been transformed into religions themselves with all the typical
religious apparatus of deified leaders, inspired bibles, and irrational,
fanatical enthusiasms.

Religion is essentially a mode of feeling and not a matter of
intellect. This is why religious apologetics leave such an unpleasant
taste in the mouth, since the apologetic writer is not using the intellect on its own plane and according to its own laws, but is forcibly
constraining it to justify beliefs held on quite other grounds. The
stultification of the intellect by constraint gives rise to the feeling
of fundamental dishonesty that always assails us when we peruse
such writings.

On the other hand, when the intellect is allowed to function
alone, abstracted upon its own level, we get philosophy with its
purely intellectual truth and its lack of influence over the rest of the
human psyche. The failure of the philosopher to put his philosophy
to any practical use is proverbial and arises from this very fact,
namely, that the feeling aspect of the psyche, not having been con-
sulted in the framing of the philosophy, will not allow its forces to be
used for its support in actual life, so that, for all his lofty thought, the
philosopher is only too often forced back in practice upon instinctive, feeling-prompted actions that may be utterly at variance with
his philosophy. Hence the accusation of sterility in practice that has
always been brought by the common man against philosophy.

In the case of the ordinary, orthodoxly religious man, the pseudo-
intellectual structure, if any, that he has raised is plainly a falsity,
his actions being motivated by feeling of the specific type we call
religious. But it is just here that his difficulty lies. Religious feeling,
as Jung has somewhere pointed out, wells up from springs that are

both muddy and clear. On the one hand there is the source in the super-mental level of the *buddhi** and, on the other hand, there is that which arises from the sub-mental desire-nature. The former feelings lead to unity and self-transcendence, while the latter drag man deep into the bog of mere animality. Hence the paradoxical behaviour characteristic of many religious men, at one moment soaring to an empyrean of devotion and self-sacrifice, at another, sinking to sub-human levels of cruelty and bestiality.

The only means of discriminating between these feelings is to be found in the mind which forms a neutral point between the two. If properly used and disciplined, the mind is capable of separating these feelings from each other and of refusing the assent of the will to the one sort, while yielding it freely to the other, of rejecting the bestial (though definitely 'religious') feeling that men get through participating in such acts as blood sacrifice and religious murder, while encouraging the higher religious feelings of love, compassion, and self-sacrifice.

The ordinary religious man, however, through having constrained his mind to the justification of *any* feeling that has the 'religious' sanction of tradition, or that is approved by 'our holy scriptures', has lost the power of such discrimination, and yields himself to the lower with as much abandon as to the higher; indeed, with more, for it makes less demands upon him. This characteristic is particularly noticeable in religious crowds whose 'sacred' ferocity has been the cause of many deeds of horror from which even the individuals who shared in them must have afterwards shrunk. Lastly, when the vested interests of priesthoods conceive themselves to be involved in the maintenance of such sub-human piety, we get the abominations of persecution and the Inquisition, while, in other quarters, the cry is raised of '*écrasez l'infame*'.

In the *Kathopanishad* the body of man is described under the figure of a chariot. Of that chariot, *buddhi* is the charioteer, mind the reins, and the *indriyas* or senses (including the desire-nature which energizes them) are the horses. The chariot will only travel properly when all these are used correctly, when the *buddhi*-guided mind restrains and directs the exuberant energy of the horses. Ordinary

*The higher intelligence, sometimes equated with intuition (Ed).

religion dispenses with the reins and makes no, or at least insufficient, distinction between the feelings that are rooted in the *buddhi* and those that belong to the desire-nature; and, whenever the latter have the specifically 'religious' quality or can claim the sanction of a 'sacred' tradition, the horses are allowed to run away with the chariot and tradition is substituted for the reins of mind.

Academic philosophy, on the other hand, tends to retire into a universe of abstract truth, discarding the element of feeling as prejudicial to the exercise of pure reason. This is like continuing to play with the reins while the bits have been removed from the horse's mouth. The occupant of the chariot abandons himself to wonderful dreams about the journey he is making, while the horses nibble the grass by the roadside or scamper wildly in the fields with their contemplative passenger.

Thus neither religion nor philosophy, as these are ordinarily understood, can be sufficient by itself, the former because it subordinates the mind to the feelings indiscriminately – or to tradition, which is another name for the same thing – and the latter because its mental workings are detached from the great instinctive driving powers of life. It is for this reason that a union of philosophy and religion is so essential, a union in which the mental discipline of the former shall control and purify the instinctive-traditional feelings of religion, while the latter shall energize the lifeless intellectual structures of philosophy. Only when this is accomplished shall we see a philosophy which actually influences life and a religion which neither sinks into abysses of 'holy' sensuality nor indulges in cruelty in the name of the service of God.

One of the greatest snares in the religious world is the delusive ideal of orthodoxy. The unorthodox Hindu, Buddhist, Muslim, and Christian are able to meet together in friendship and mutual respect even in the religious sphere. They are willing not only to live and let live, but also to sympathize with each other's faiths, to try to understand them, and even to learn from mutual interchange. Once, however, the demon of orthodoxy raises its ugly head, all this harmony disappears. It doesn't matter which of these great religions the man belongs to, as soon as he becomes infected by the desire to be orthodox, he erects a barrier between himself and his fellows. It is true that the barriers of some orthodoxies are more prickly and forbidding than those of others, but essentially they are all the same: those within are true believers, and the rest are infidels, *mlecchas*, heathens, *Kafirs*, or *tirthikas*.

Not only with regard to other religions, even within the limits of a given religion, orthodoxy sets up barriers and creates ill-feeling. The more orthodox a Roman Catholic is, the more he hates Protestants, and the more orthodox a *Vaishnava*, the less he will have to do with *Shaivas*. Thus each religion gets split up into a number of conflicting sects, though it should be obvious that this process decreases the probability of truth being found in any of them, since, the smaller the sect, the less likely would it seem to be that it alone should possess the truth while all the rest wander in error.

The fact that orthodoxy thus sets barriers between man and man is an excellent reason for its avoidance, since all such dividers of human unity drag the soul deeper and deeper into the power of the great divider, matter. He who would lead the spiritual life must learn to assimilate himself increasingly to the fundamental nature of Spirit, which is Unity.

Moreover, if we glance at the conditions under which any of the great orthodoxies have arisen, we shall see that there are also very good reasons why that which is orthodox should never be the truth, and vice versa. For, what is the process? A great seer arises, one whose wisdom so far exceeds that of ordinary men that the latter are apt to consider him a God. In truth, he is but a man, as all are, save that he lives no longer in the separate ego, but in that divine and all-pervading Spirit which is the ever living heart of all that is, and he has thus become an incarnation of its wisdom.

Such a divine seer imparts to all men whatever they are able to receive of his wisdom, but, since capacities differ, he by no means teaches all in the same manner. All teaching is in symbols, and not only will the symbols used vary from hearer to hearer according to their differing types and needs, but also the meaning of those self-same symbols will vary according to the degree of the hearer's spiritual insight. We read, for instance, that when Buddha addressed a crowd of men, each of them felt that the words were addressed peculiarly to him alone. That was because the words of such a teacher, springing as they did from the depths of the universal spirit, touched something deep in each man's heart so that they seemed specially adapted to his own personal problems and difficulties. All who have had the good fortune to listen to a real seer, even though a less exalted one than Christ or a Buddha, will have noticed this phenomenon which is rooted in the very nature of spiritual insight and so is strictly universal.

But then the seer withdraws from his personal ego to live for ever in that selfless Spirit which is the one true Self. As we crudely put it, he dies, and his disciples see him no more. They collect together to memorize or write down the teachings they heard from his lips when he was with them. We must never forget that we do not possess the actual teachings of the founders, but only such of them as were handed down by their followers and formed into canons, or orthodox bodies of scripture. And it is just here that the difficulty begins. Men of deep spiritual insight are always rare, and the deeper the insight, the rarer it will be. The majority of the disciples will be men of ordinary insight, and their voices will prevail at the councils called to determine the faith. Speaking more accurately, the men who come to the front and whose opinions prevail at such councils – we can actually see the progress at work in the history of both Buddhism and Christianity – will be those men who, while possessed of more than average strength of character and *intellect*, yet have the same degree and type of *spiritual* insight as has the ordinary disciple, and so can satisfy the latter by giving to his feelings a coherency and an incisiveness that he himself would not have been able to attain. The Christian Gnostics, the inheritors of Christ's inner teachings, divided men into three types which they termed *hylic*, *psychic*, and *pneumatic*, those whose inner values were material, emotional-mental, and spiritual, respectively. Among any body of disciples it will be the middle one of these types that is most numerous, a fact which is as true of the disciples of a present-day teacher as it was in the past.

The opinions of the relatively few men of deep spiritual insight, the *pneumatikoi*, will therefore receive scant attention at the councils, the forces of jealousy adding their sinister quota to the innocent depreciation caused by failure to understand. The inevitable result will be that those few who have the deepest understanding of the master's teachings will either be forced into silence or else expelled from the church as heretical. This is what happened to the Gnostics, who were expelled, persecuted, and finally stamped out by the Catholic orthodoxy, simply because their understanding was too deep for the average church father. It appears also to have happened at the second council of the Buddhists at which it would seem that those who understood most of the spirit of the Buddha were forced to secede and separately hand on the traditions which afterwards became the *Mahāyāna*. (The orthodox account makes the split depend upon certain petty matters of monastic descipline, but then that is the orthodox account.) Not only is there reason to suppose that this is what did happen; there is reason to know that it is what *must* have happened and must always happen, since it is a process based on the universal characteristics of human nature.

There is no question here of an actual esoteric doctrine imparted only by a few chosen disciples. That is a further problem with which we are not just now concerned. All we have to note here is that spiritual insight is inevitably esoteric and aristocratic, while the councils held to determine orthodoxy are democratic and popular. Some one perhaps objects that the Buddhist councils were composed of *Arhats*, enlightened seers. Yes, yes; and the Christian ones were composed of saints, but let that pass. Those who do not wish to see will never see; but it should be obvious to anyone of intelligence that the process described above is inevitable while human nature is what it is, and that the inevitable result is the creation of a body of ortho-dox doctrine and interpretation which satisfies the man of mediocre spiritual insight just because it was created by such and for such.

It is no less obvious that it is useless to expect to find the deepest spiritual truths in these established churches. The latter are tolerably suited to the needs of the ordinary religious man who uses his religion mainly as a lubricant to help him over the roughnesses of life. Beyond that they are of little use, except is so far as their rituals and symbols unknowingly preserve ancient and forgotten traditions, much as the rocks preserve the fossils of extinct forms of life. Their claim to possess the Truth is false, and their quarrels with each other are childish, resembling nothing so much as the disputes of small boys about the importance of their respective fathers' places in the world, a matter of which they know nothing whatever. Even the lubricating oil they furnish for the average man has to be paid for heavily because of the obscurantism and selfish cunning found in priesthoods who raise the cry 'our holy religion is in danger', when all that is in truth endangered is their own comfortable position in human society.

The seeker after spiritual knowledge, the traveller on the real inner Path, should begin to look about him with very wide open eyes if he finds himself lying in the bed of orthodoxy, a bed which only too often is one of those sinister constructions found in some medieval inns, the canopy of which descended in the night, smothering the unfortunate wayfarer beneath its weight. The only safe place for the traveller of this Path is the open road of the heart, the only safe shelter, that of the limitless sky. Travelling thus, like a true *Sannyās** with no baggage to encumber him, seeking no security beyond that of his own Self, demanding nothing of Gods or men, but content with whatever comes, avoiding the crowded haunts of men and never wasting a day by lingering in the comfort of yesterday's halting place, in this way faring onward, ever northward, guided by the light of the pole star, he will assuredly reach the fixed abode and see the midnight sun that shines in darkness. There and there only will he find the true religion, reflected gleams of whose Light gave whatever life they possessed to the creeds he has left behind, a religion which existed before men were on this earth, one in which there are neither churches, priests, nor God, since nothing that is pointed out for worship can be the one true root of all that is.

Man's extremity has been said to be God's opportunity. If that were altogether true, the Deific morals would have a rather dubious flavour and be something like those of a prison chaplain who plies his wares to a man who is just completing a spell of solitary confinement. Yet it is certainly a fact that in times of extremity men do turn to religion, if only as a frightened child runs to its mother's lap to receive a soothing caress and the assurance that all is well.

On the other hand, the philosopher with a toothache is notorious. His philosophy deserts him, or, rather, he deserts his philosophy

*A Hindu wandering mendicant monk.

and ramps about the house, showing in his pain rather less self-control than the ordinary man who has never toyed with ideas that pleasure and pain are mere illusions of the senses. Why is it that in periods of stress religion grows stronger and affords a welcome, if often largely superstitious, support, while philosophy is apt to be a reed which breaks in the hand?

The reason is that, while for most men philosophy is a matter of the intellect alone, religion throws down deep roots into our instinctive life. Do not men learn their religion at their mothers' knees, and is it not only natural that a terrible and hostile world should send men back to those same knees for protection?

For philosophy, however, there are no such easily attained protective arms, but a stern call to the facing of facts as they are. There can be no appeal to the 'mysterious ways' of an inscrutable providence, but only a determined enquiry into the nature of the horror, a tracing of the evil to its roots in our own hearts, and, if the philosophy is to be more than the academic intellectualism nowadays dignified by that name, a steady effort to destroy those roots. This is a task for grown-up men; and there is still too much of the child in our natures for it to be an easy one for us. To see this we have only to note how, under the stress of illness, sometimes even a trifling cold in the head, our behaviour takes on the fretful and peevish characteristics of a spoilt child.

Religious preachers are never tired of expatiating on the contrast we have just sketched, though the moral they draw from it is not altogether the one which we ourselves are drawing. Nevertheless, the fact remains that no religious martyr, dying in the supporting arms of a fanatical faith, has surpassed the calm heroism with which the philosopher Socrates went willingly to an unjust death, entering the waters of the gloomy and terrible river with such a quiet and manful dignity that the beholders must have felt, if they could not actually see, his safe arrival on the other shore.

Clearly, it is not philosophy that is to blame, but philosophers. It is because our philosophy is an affair of our heads and not of our hearts that it is for us so often a broken reed. We construct 'systems', or, more usually, merely criticize the systems of others; we manipulate the pallid abstractions that we call ideas; proclaim that the real is the rational and the rational the real; assert that the objects of the world around us are 'only' ideas, or, going to the other extreme, deny reality to anything that is not perceptible to our senses. But it is not so. The real is far more than the merely rational, the world far more than mere 'ideas', while sense experience is but a picking up of ocean flotsam. Ideas are no more the whole of reality that a railway time-table is the railway, and sense experience is no more the entire world than the flotsam on the surface of the waves is the whole content of the fathomless ocean. From those waves some seek refuge in the parental arms of emotional religion: 'God's in his heaven, all's well with the world'; others in the textbook mentalism of a purely intellectual philosophy: 'These trenches are not on my map – they can't be real'. Both alike are haunted by the demons they fear to face, the former by the lurking doubts that, after all, the divine protecting arms are but 'Human – all too human', the latter by the thunder of great tidal waves that find no mention in the official almanac.

It is not behind emotional or intellectual defence mechanisms that we can find security; it is in the open that we must meet our foes. Man's strength is in the soul, and he who would stand firm amid the tides of fear and sorrow must seek and find the pathway to that soul. If religion or philosophy are to be of any real importance, they must be such as will set our feet on that pathway, and must give us comforting beliefs, not intellectual opinions, not even firmly adhered to convictions, but that inner and certain Knowledge that burns up sorrow as the fire consumes chaff. That divine Knowledge of the soul, that penetrating insight into the nature of things as they are, into the modes of their arising and their passing away, that Knowledge exists now as it has always done. Now, as in ancient times, there are those who have mastered it in all its fullness; now, as always, there are those whose eyes are learning painfully to open to its divine light. Religious traditions or philosophical adventurings that can give us any guidance to that Path are the most valuable possessions of the human race; their study and even their mere preservation are among the most valuable of all human activities. As for the rest, the philosophy and religion that are mere refuges from reality, the religion that is a parental head-patting for a frightened child, and the philosophy that is a mere arena for academic gymnastics, all these have little if anything to do with that Pathway. They are mere actions and reactions of the human personality, having as much real significance as Turkish baths and crossword puzzles.

Let us look into our hearts and say in which category our own philosophy and religion are to be found.

Philosophy and religion are the two modes under which the human psyche apprehends the universe. They are the most general manifestations of the thinking and feeling functions respectively, and they must be wedded to each other if the resulting apprehension is to be a healthy and harmoniously developed offspring.

It will be seen that we understand the terms philosophy and religion in a somewhat wider sense than is current nowadays. Science, for instance, is most essentially a mode of mental apprehension, but we have made no separate mention of it. It is only quite recently that the one-sided mentalism of our age has allowed science to arrogate to itself the title of *scientia* or knowledge *par excellence* and to set up house independently. Previous to that, under the name of natural philosophy, it lived happily, as it were, in a joint family, and its setting up for itself of an establishment of its own is only an example of the unfortunate separatism of the age in which we live.

Had science not been so eager to proclaim itself an entirely independent mode of knowledge, we should not have seen so frequently the lamentable spectacle of scientists writing about 'matter' and 'causation' as if Hume and similar thinkers had never written their critiques of those notions. We should, in fact, have had less of that ignorant scorn for metaphysic that is constantly betraying scientists into writing nonsense, for 'No metaphysics is simply bad metaphysics'.* Moreover, had science not yielded to the separatist spirit of the times, it might have been less ready than it now so often is to prostitute itself before the lecherous nationalist idols, and mankind thus would have been spared much suffering and more shame. By separating itself from the main tree, science has definitely weakened everything except its egotism.

Just as science or natural philosophy is a special branch with special aims and methods of that mental apprehension of the uni-

*Bertram Keightley.

verse which constitutes philosophy in general, so art, which has also disastrously enlarged its ego at the expense of truth and harmony, is a branch of the feeling mode which is what we understand by religion. Here again, parental dogmatism was the root cause of the split. Those who sat in the seats of the hierophants had nothing 'sacred' or otherwise to show, and the artist who, in India, Egypt, and China, as well as in medieval Europe, had been a happy son of the temple, was forced to start a sect of his own if he would escape sterility.

As for the philosophical and religious pontiffs who sit on the academic and ecclesiastical thrones, they whose mouths are grey with mumbling the dust of a thousand books, their days are numbered. Jung remarked that the universities were ceasing to be centres of light, and, assuredly, few now think of consulting the ecclesiastics on any important matter. It is they, the pontiffs of both sorts, whose learned dogmatism has shattered the unity of the Tree of Knowledge; but even now a wind is stirring in the unsleeping depths of the psyche which will blow them away and scatter their dust to the four quarters. Only when this has been accomplished will it be possible again for the true hierophants to show forth the sacred mysteries of life and death, and for the Tree of Knowledge to put forth once more its unity of foliage from its buried but undecaying roots.

The penalty which has to be paid for fission in the psyche is neurosis; and just as the grey and lifeless materialism of the age is the price we pay for the scientific secession, so the phantasies of contemporary and allied cults are the neurosis which results from the artistic one. The psyche is one and, though divisible, is not with impunity to be divided. To think grey thoughts about the universe, or to luxuriate in warm but purely personal feelings, is no substitute for its integral apprehension by the psyche as a whole.

It is well that we should find time to pause and remember that the world as a thing in itself has no existence. We mean that there is no such thing as a solid globe of earth, spinning its way on an orbit round another globe called the sun in a detached, self-existing, and quite impersonal manner. Notwithstanding all that may be written by scientists upon the nature of such a globe, there is no such thing.

The name earth is given to a certain way of looking at reality, a certain partial integration of reality, made under the forces of desire and therefore springing from ignorance. The descriptions of it as a globe and as moving on an elliptical orbit are convenient schematizations of our experience, but they are no more than that and should not be taken as such. Springing out of it, they are tainted by the ignorance which gave them birth.

The very ground under our feet supports us not because of any inherent 'solidity' it possesses in its own right, but because it is a misperception of the all-supporting *Brahman*. This was the lesson which the Gods were taught by the mysterious *Yaksha* (the Supreme or Absolute Being) in the *Kenopanishad*. Without the hidden power, *Agni* (Fire) could not burn a straw nor *Vayu* (Air) blow it away. 'They went at it with all speed', but were unable to accomplish anything at all.

We have been told that because of the *Ātman* earth supports, water moistens, and fire burns. We have been told this; we piously repeat it on suitable occasions; but we do not believe it, and, whenever possible, we forget it. Forget is just the word. All forgetting is more or less deliberate. We forget a thing because we do not wish to remember. In other words, forgetting springs from desire.

What desire? In this case the desire for personal safety, the desire to establish our illusory personal egos firmly and, so to say, on the solid earth, in a world that is changing around us at every moment. It is this desire that leads us to see the seamless garment of reality as a thing of shreds and patches, as cut up into so many stable, or at least relatively stable, objects which by their mere enduring can reassure us that we too endure. This is why we like to surround ourselves with a host of familiar objects and why, the older we get, the more apt we are to dislike their being changed or broken. Their impermanence reminds us too painfully of our own essential transiency.

But there are no such objects in reality. There is no earth, no water, no air, no fire. There is no floor on which we sit, no paper on which we write, no hand which guides the pen, no separate self which guides the hand. This is neither 'philosophy' nor poetic rhapsody, but just truth. All these things have sprung out of the desire for stability, and that desire is based on ignorance, because only the *Brahman* is stable (*dhruva*) and only in that *Brahman* can we find the fixed abode which we ignorantly and hopelessly seek elsewhere.

Deep within us there is that which knows this. Our superficial ignorance of it is 'a sleep and a forgetting', and we forget it just because we wish to live a life of separated selfishness. All such wishes are doomed to ultimate frustration because they go against the nature of reality which is one without a second. If we assert the right to live as separate beings (and we can make this assertion just because in us is the power and freedom of the *Ātman* which is our heart) we must pay for it by being tied fast to the chariot wheels of Fate. As Christ said to Peter, we gird ourselves to go whither we wish and, in the end, we are bound by another to be taken whither we wish not.

Lightly we leap into the sunny air of separate life, and heavily do we fall back into the dark waters of death. This is the wheel, 'the weary, the misery laden'.* But, as the Buddha states in Arnold's poem, we are not truly bound. The wheel has no reality for, in truth, separation itself is unreal.

By our desires we have ourselves created that gloomy wheel on which ourselves are broken. That wheel we call 'the world', but it is nothing at all, nothing but a phantom, called into being by the wand of desire. Moreover, the nature of the phantom while it lasts – and this is the important thing for us to remember – corresponds to the nature of the desires that called it forth.

The world we live in today may *seem* to be quite different from the sort of world we would have wished to live in, but it is not so. We look only at the bright and sunny front of our desires, turning away hurriedly from their dark and gloomy backs. But all things are twofold. If they have a brightly lit front, they have a back which is correspondingly dark. This is the inevitable nature of manifestation. No artificialities of flood-lighting can remove the shadow. The artificially bright scenes of the theatre, for instance, have a behind of quite particular ugliness.

Therefore we say that the world in which we are at present living is the exact correspondence of our desires, if those desires be seen in their entirety. We cannot desire in terms of violence, even if of only mental violence, without having that violence thrust back upon us by the phantoms we have created. All worlds whatsoever

*From the Orphic Tablets.

are worlds of sorrow (*dukkha*) in some form, because all worlds are called into being by desire. This present world of ours, so particularly hideous with murder and destruction, is the inevitable result of the lamentably unbalanced nature of modern life. This is shown in the way in which the destruction particularly affects those filthy ant-heaps that we call our great cities, for it is in them that life has taken on its most unbalanced forms.

Neither is it of any use to protest our innocence and to lay, as is our wont, the blame on the other fellow. What we have not had a hand in the making of cannot impinge on us at all. It is true that there are degrees of individual responsibility in the matter, but there are also corresponding degrees in the extent to which the resultant situation impinges upon us. There is no luck or chance about the process, but only the unerring hand of *Karma*. As a man sows, so shall he reap; and he who wields the sword of violence in his thoughts shall see that sword menacing him from the so-called outer world, the world which is made up of the phantoms we ourselves have evoked.

'This is the Truth; as from a blazing fire shoot forth thousands of sparks, so from the imperishable issue forth all beings and to it they return.'*

What is the wind that blows them forth? It is the wind of desire. From that wind and its resultant effects there is no shelter in any of the phantom worlds, but only in that of which Gaudapāda has written: 'There is no destruction and no coming into being, none who is bound, none who strives, no seeker after liberation, none who is liberated. This is the Highest Truth.'

'Whoever desires to be a practical philosopher,' said the great Paracelsus, 'ought to be able to indicate heaven and hell in the microcosm and to find everything in Man that exists in heaven or on earth. He must be able to turn the exterior into the interior. But this is an art which he can only acquire by experience and by the Light of nature which is shining before the eyes of every man, but which is seen by few mortals.'

This universal teaching of the seers was well known to the writers of the Upanishads, as also to the *Tāntrik* schools who placed the seven worlds and all their denizens within this six-foot human

*Mundaka Upanishad.

frame. It is a teaching, however, which modern man tends to turn away from. If he is a philosopher, he looks at it askance as a relic of God-knows-what ancient superstition, and he prefers to busy himself with formal enquiries into the nature of sense-data or the structure of logical propositions. Ask him what is within man, and, after quibbling for an hour or so on the meaning of 'within', he will say that in all probability and according to the views of Professor Tweedledum there is something abstract termed a mind, but that it is just possible that Professor Tweedledum may be right in holding that the so-called mind is only a complex of conditioned reflexes. As for anything else that may be within us, he will politely refer us to the doctor.

Nor will the religious man be found much more helpful. The age-old hostility between the priest and the magician still makes itself felt, if only subconsciously, and he feels that religion should be a matter of simple faith in a benevolent providence, nourished, perhaps, by some thin gruel of intellectual theism. Heaven and hell? Oh yes, after death, no doubt, heaven for me and hell for you! All very proper, but don't let us talk of such depressing subjects. What is within man? His immortal soul, *Ātmā*, or what not. What is that soul? Well, we don't really know, but it is something very spiritual, too spiritual in fact to be described. The interview concludes with the offer of a loan of his particular sacred scriptures for us to study.

As for the practical man, he looks for truth in telescopes and microscopes, in millions and millionths, and in laboratory wonders in general. He will, of course, refer us at once to the doctor who is himself writ large and who, with knife in one hand and stethoscope in the other, will give us an answer which amounts in the end to what the nursery rhyme called 'slugs and snails and puppy-dog's tails'. Paracelsus? Yes, he was a member of our profession and a great man in his day – discovered the circulation of the blood or the stagnation of the bile, I can't quite remember which – and no doubt by heaven and hell he simply meant health and disease.

It seems there is no one willing to take Paracelsus seriously; yet the latter was giving utterance to a truth which is of the utmost practical importance and which at one time was understood by the wise of all nations. It is ignorance of this truth that is responsible for the mist of unreality which has spread over all modern learning.

What Paracelsus termed the light of nature has, since his time, been hidden even more zealously behind a rampart of books in front of which the scientist, as high priest of this age, peers through telescope or microscope at meaningless stars above him or meaningless atoms beneath, while religion and philosophy perch on his shoulders, nodding wisely at each other, like two owls.

But Paracelsus was entirely right. There is a sun above us in the heavens, and there is also a sun within these mortal frames. Sun, moon, and planets weave their intricate patterns in the sky above us, and no less do they weave them in the tissues of our bodies and in the subtler tissues of our psyches. . . . Within us are all the Gods, and without their power not the slightest movement of our little finger, not the most conditioned of conditioned reflexes could take place. The Gods, we repeat, shine above us in the sky, and the same Gods shine within us in the ether of the heart. As Thales said, 'all things are full of Gods', and on a knowledge of their hierarchies must be based all true sciences and all true arts, all philosophy and all religion. From the Gods comes healing for the body, from the same Gods healing for the soul. From them comes knowledge of past and future, from them the power to mould the living present.

Long ago this great truth was known to all men, consciously to the wise few and instinctively to the many. We have forgotten it, and this forgetfulness is the deep-rooted cause of all our modern unrest. Only when we re-discover the Gods in ourselves shall we be able once again to see them in the outer world as well. Only then shall we become what Paracelsus terms practical philosophers, and only then shall we attain once more to that inner and outer harmony of being that we have lost. Only then, too, will theology cease to be the tissue of empty words which it is at present and become again the Queen of the sciences, the knowledge of those shining powers whose life is manifested as this universe. Above them and below them there is nothing; above, the nothing of the divine darkness, below, the reflected nothing of matter. Between these two nothings extends the whole living web of the divine tapestry, the fabric of the universe, the gleaming garment of the divine play, the golden patterns of the ever-moving planets, circling against the background of eternal stars.